TENNIS

SKILLS
TACTICS
TECHNIQUES

CROWOOD SPORTS GUIDES

TENNIS

SKILLS
TACTICS
TECHNIQUES

Jeremy Woods

THE CROWOOD PRESS

First published in 2014 by
The Crowood Press Ltd
Ramsbury, Marlborough
Wiltshire SN8 2HR

www.crowood.com

British Library Cataloguing-in-Publication Data
A catalogue record for this book is available from the British Library.

ISBN 978 1 84797 748 9

Acknowledgements
The author and publishers wish to thank the following for their kind permission to reproduce their photographs in this book: Lauren Hamilton, Michaela Knepsl, Sasha Philbert and Dominic Tripp. Thanks also to Westside LTC, London SW19 for the use of their courts and to The Racket Specialist Shop, London SW19.

Photographs by George Powell

Dedication
To Ava and Amy (sorry for the wait!)

Throughout this book, the pronouns 'he', 'him', and 'his' have been used inclusively and are intended to apply to both males and females. Similarly, the right-handed player is used as the model for teaching technique for reasons of consistency and clarity (apologies to all left-handers!).

Typeset by Jean Cussons Typesetting, Diss, Norfolk

Printed and bound in India by Replika Press Pvt Ltd

CONTENTS

INTRODUCTION

The great thing about tennis is that it is genuinely a sport for all – whether you are six or sixty, male or female, have a lot of time to put into the game, or just have time for an occasional hit. In the same way, this book is intended to provide something of use for all tennis players, from the beginner just starting out in the game, to the committed player wishing to improve to his fullest potential.

Why is it that the game provides so much enjoyment for so many people in so many different countries and cultures? Tennis (or something very like it) has been around a long time, so its fascination for many is beyond doubt. The Roman wall paintings of Themistocles, dated around 500BC, depict athletes playing something remarkably close to the game, and the word 'tennis' itself can be traced in English writings to the year 1399 (John Gower: 'In Prise of Peace'). Obviously, the fundamentals of striking a ball with a racquet were intrinsically popular before Lawn Tennis itself was introduced to the UK in 1873 by Army Major Walter Clopton Wingfield, who called it by the (thankfully short-lived) name of 'Sphairistike'. Perhaps the answer lies in the fact that the challenge exists just as much in one's mastery of the ball as it does in the mastery of an opponent or in winning.

Like golf, we all have improvement to strive for, irrespective of our achievements in the game. The Grand Slam title winner still strives for improvement in technique that he or she knows can still be achieved, in the same way as the beginner strives to develop a consistent backhand that will keep the ball in play. The variables in tennis all provide a a tantalizingly close, but still elusive challenge. The ball, your opponent, the court surface, your level of fitness, the wind, your stamina, the spin on the ball, the pace of your shot, and so on – all combine to make the superficially simple game of tennis more like an exercise in three-dimensional chess!

Yet, marvellously, the game remains approachable by all, and not just by the top athlete or the supremely talented. I hope this book improves your performance and enjoyment of the game, no matter what your current standard might be, and I wish you good luck in a sport you can bank on enjoying for the rest of your life.

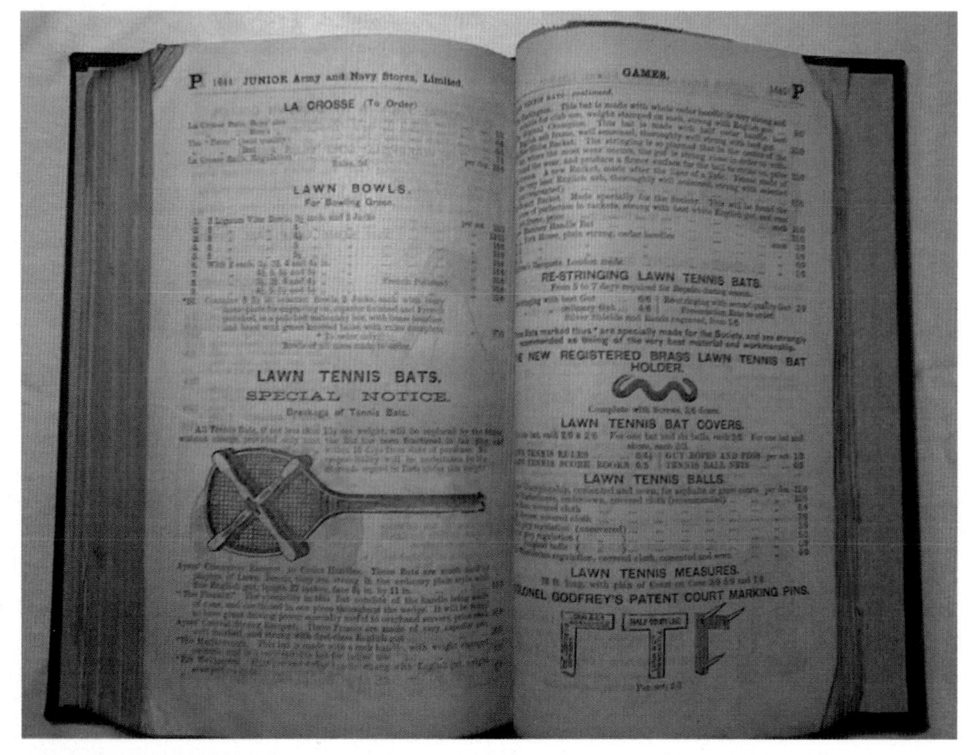

JUNIOR Army and Navy Stores, Limited

LA CROSSE (To Order)

LAWN BOWLS.

LAWN TENNIS BATS.

SPECIAL NOTICE.

GAMES.

RE-STRINGING LAWN TENNIS BATS.

NEW REGISTERED BRASS LAWN TENNIS BAT HOLDER.

LAWN TENNIS BAT COVERS.

LAWN TENNIS BALLS.

LAWN TENNIS MEASURES.

GODFREY'S PATENT COURT MARKING PINS.

A page from the UK Army and Navy Stores Catalogue *dated 1897, advertising early tennis 'bats' and court equipment.*

PART I

AN INTRODUCTION TO TENNIS

CHAPTER 1

THE RULES OF THE GAME, SIMPLIFIED

1. The object of the game, which can be played between two or four people, is to put the ball into play over the net, bouncing it within the court boundary lines in such a way that your opponent cannot return it similarly over the net into your half of the court.
2. The ball may not bounce twice before being returned, but it can be volleyed (hit before the bounce) except on service returns.
3. The server's score is always called first. Zero is referred to as 'love', the first point as 15, the second as 30, the third as 40. Thus, if the server loses the first point, it is love-15. If he loses the second also, it is love-30, etc. If the score reaches 40-all, it is referred to as 'deuce'. The next point after deuce is referred to as 'advantage'-player X. The next point will thus be either game-player X, or it will revert to deuce, as a game must be won by two clear points.
4. A player who first wins six games wins a 'set', except that he must win by a margin of two clear games. Matches are normally the best of three, or sometimes five, sets.
5. Tie-break games were introduced to beat the deadlock caused by strong servers with the resultant marathon matches. They normally take place at 6 games all, except when the final set, or what may be the final set, is taking place. The player who was due to serve next starts by serving the first point; his opponent then serves for the second and third points, and this pattern continues with each player serving for two points at a time. The first player to win by 7 points (provided it's by a 2-point lead) wins the set. At every multiple of 6 points, the players change ends, in order to

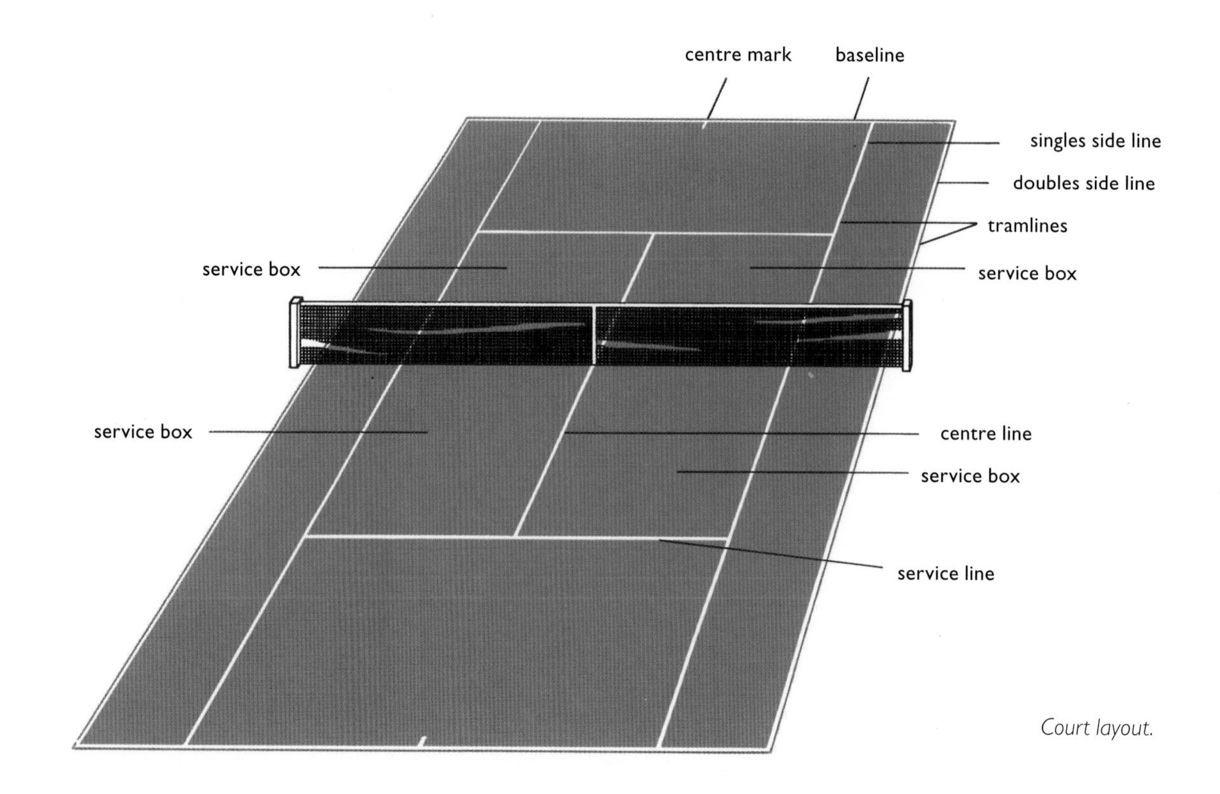

Court layout.

share the benefits or disadvantages caused by sun and wind, etc. The player who serves first in the tie-break is considered to be using his service turn, so when play resumes in the next set with normal scoring, his opponent serves first. In some tournaments, a 'champions' tie-break' may be played. This follows the same format as a regular tie-break, except the winner is the first to 10 points with 2 points clear.

6. To serve, the server stands facing his opponent behind the baseline and to the right of the centre mark. He then places the ball into the air and strikes it, before it bounces, over the net and into his opponent's diagonally opposite serving box. The server gets two goes at serving each point. If he fails, it is called a 'double fault', and he loses the point. If he strikes a serve that his opponent cannot even reach, it's called an 'ace'. If the ball touches the top of the net on the service and still drops in, it's called a 'let', and the server has another go. If the server's foot touches the line or the inside of the court before he hits the ball, it's called a 'foot fault'. Service points are played alternately from each side of the centre mark, diagonally across court. At the end of each game, the opposing player becomes the server.
7. When a game ends and the score is an uneven number, i.e. 1-love or 3-2, players change ends.
8. If play is interfered with (perhaps by a ball rolling across the court from a nearby game) a let is called and the point is played again. Players should familiarize themselves with the complete rules of tennis, published by the International Tennis Federation (see Appendix).

RULES CHECK

You are not foot-faulting unless you touch the service line with your foot before you make contact with the ball.

CHAPTER 2

GETTING STARTED: CLOTHES AND EQUIPMENT

If you're starting from scratch, you can be up and running for tennis in no time at all. All you need are a limited number of absolute essentials, and you are ready. With racquet, strings, balls, shoes, clothes, court and opponent, you have all you need. Add a little coaching if you like, join a club, enter tournaments, and you are really on your way.

Choosing a Racquet

Choosing a new racquet can be a daunting experience. Oversized heads, ceramic fibres, wide bodies, long bodies, micro-density stringing – where to start? Fortunately, it is not as complicated as all that. Racquets have come a long way from the old one-size, one-material (wood) days, but the criteria for choosing one haven't changed much at all. Basically, you should be concerned with durability, weight and balance, stiffness relative to your style of play, grip size and the relationship between price and value.

This is not a problem with today's generation of racquets. New generation composite materials are being constantly developed to improve performance, so today's frames are more likely to be changed because of the dictates of marketing and fashion rather than because they become damaged. However, no racquet will take kindly for too long to being hammered on the ground in anger or scraped too frequently when picking up balls.

Racquet Types

There are basically three kinds of racquets: one for the Junior, one for the Power or Game Improver and one for the Control Player (these are sometimes called 'Players' racquets)

Junior racquets come in a variety of sizes and are designed to fit the needs of the growing child according to his or her relative height.

Power/Game Improver racquets tend to have outsized or oversized heads (being typically 107–135sq. in.). They tend towards lightness (8–9.5oz), are sometimes longer than normal (27–29in. long) and are balanced with the weight somewhat towards the head or evenly balanced.

Choosing a new racquet can be a daunting experience.

Control/Players racquets, by contrast, tend to be heavier (11.5–13oz) with a smaller head (85–98sq. in.), standard length, and weighted slightly towards a 'head light' feel.

Weight and Balance

Weight and balance are vital ingredients in your choice, but can be misleading. A lighter frame may actually feel great, while providing insufficient mass in the head and consequential loss of power. In very general terms, it is better to go for a slightly head-heavy model that will actually do some of the work for you and be easier on the body, as it provides more fluid strokes. Players with shorter swings on their ground strokes, though, may find a Power/Game Improver frame a better choice. In general then, you should choose a weight that feels comfortable to you, and avoid anything that feels unbalanced in the head. Always ask the advice of your tennis coach or local racquet retailer.

Stiffness

Stiffness has increased massively in frames since the days of wooden racquets. First, materials like graphite and Kevlar paved the way, then the new wide-body frames stiffened up the racquets even more. Sorbothane and Sensathane were introduced by manufacturers to act as vibration preventers and it quickly became possible to use a very stiff frame without any ill effects. Bigger, stronger players should opt for stiffer, heavier frames, as their long powerful strokes will sky the ball if played with a flexible racquet. Frame stiffness doesn't only affect power, though. Control and comfort are also at stake as stiffer racquets don't deflect as much on impact, resulting in less power drain than a flexible racquet. Racquet frames absorb energy, either more or less, according to stiffness.

Consequently, there has to be a trade-off between power and control. Stiff racquets might be too powerful for some advanced players to control and flexible racquets might have the same impact on a beginner or intermediate player. The degree of comfort experienced will also be affected by stiffness, and players with sore shoulders or arm injuries will generally be advised to use a very stiff frame. Again, ask advice before buying.

Grip Size

This is easy to determine, and should provide comfort allied with control. Two easy methods for determining grip size are as follows:

First, hold the racquet normally, and place the index finger of your free hand between the ball of your thumb and the fingertips of your playing hand. If it fits comfortably, the grip size is OK. Second, measure the distance between the end of your racquet-hand ring-finger and the middle of your palm. This distance corresponds to the racquet sizes 1–5 shown on the accompanying chart. Thus, if in the diagram the distance A–B = $4\frac{3}{8}$", the correct size of grip would be size 3.

Price

Price is difficult to generalize on. There are a lot of cheap racquets around but they are often of poor quality and won't help your game. On the other hand, the most expensive frames are probably totally unnecessary for the vast majority of players. As with most things, the truth lies somewhere in between. Many top players have achieved World No. 1 rankings with frames recognized as being in the value-for-money, middle-end range of the retail market. In general, it is probably true to say that you get what you pay for.

In short, remember that success with any racquet is probably 90 per cent mental and 10 per cent physical. The important thing is to get a frame that you feel happy with. Therefore, do your research thoroughly. There are numerous excellent websites that will provide you with a comprehensive list of racquets available. Ask your coach. Try and playtest your shortlist before making a final decision or, failing that, at least make some practice swings and get the feel of the frame. Most good retailers will allow you to playtest racquets before buying, usually on provision of a credit card

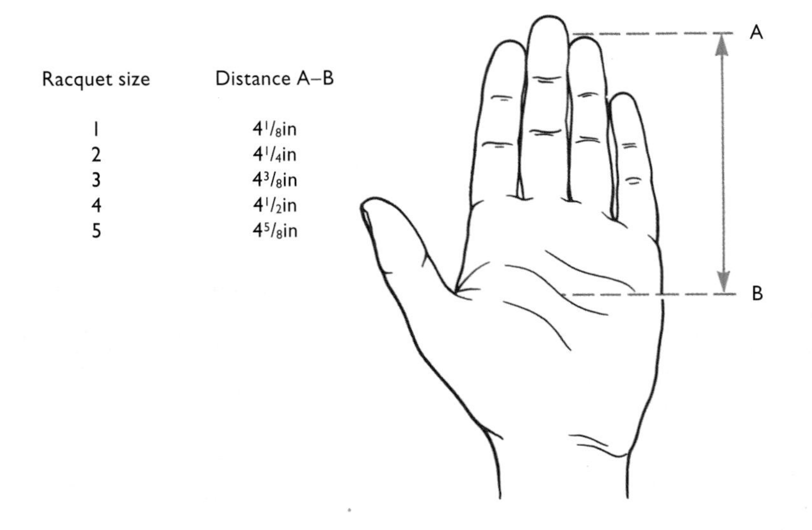

Racquet size	Distance A–B
1	$4\frac{1}{8}$in
2	$4\frac{1}{4}$in
3	$4\frac{3}{8}$in
4	$4\frac{1}{2}$in
5	$4\frac{5}{8}$in

Measuring your grip.

deposit. A satisfied buyer means a future balls and equipment purchaser for them!

Strings

Although most off-the-shelf racquets are bought ready-strung, the actual strings employed in these frames are often of inferior quality, or the frames have been strung so long (sitting on a factory shelf before the retailer's shelf) that they have lost their tension and resilience. Generally, a playable string will snap back quickly upon ball impact. For this reason, it is always advisable to buy your racquet unstrung (particularly so if you are an experienced player) as the frame's playability may be seriously compromised by the quality of the strings already in it.

When it comes to selecting the best strings for your frame and for your game, be guided by your stringing expert. Basically the choice lies between gut (which is manufactured from the smooth muscle portion of sheep, or from cow intestines) and a range of synthetics that include nylon, Kevlar, oil-filled, graphite string, polyester, artificial gut, etc. Each string has its own characteristic. For example, Kevlar is extremely durable but very stiff, so it is often combined with nylon (on the horizontals) to soften it a little and enhance control. Research has shown that gut gives greater pace to a ball than nylon when the same level of tension is used, but on the other hand it is not as durable as the synthetics because of its lower tensile strength. (Gut has an average tensile strength of 128 pounds while synthetics average between 160 and 175 pounds.)

Irrespective of the type of string purchased, you should be aware of the characteristics of low and high tension strung racquets. Generally speaking, a higher tension will contribute to control by causing an embedding of the strings into the ball, while a lower tension will cause the ball to deform less and therefore lose less energy, thus giving more power to the shot. Similarly, thinner strings allow for more feel on the ball, while thicker strings give more durability and are therefore good for clay courts, where breakage occurs more often due to the relative heaviness of the ball and the friction caused by loose court dressing abrading the string. All racquets have a recommended string tension range supplied by the manufacturer and it is a good idea to experiment within this range in order to find the ideal tension for your style of play.

Some players also prefer to insert a small rubber dampener into the strings just at the point where the lowest horizontal meets the middle of the verticals. This has the effect of taking out some of the natural vibration that occurs in the frame on impact with the ball. Remember, though, that if you use one of these, it may not touch more than one (your lowest) horizontal string, otherwise you are breaking the ITF rules of the game.

The range of choice in string type is now huge, and probably the best advice is to playtest a variety of strings in order to determine what is best for your game. While gut undoubtedly has the edge for power, control and resilience, it is ruined by playing in the rain and is by far the most expensive option. You should be prepared for a lot of restrings during the year if gut is your choice.

You should be prepared to restring your racquet.

In point of fact, you should be prepared to restring your racquet as many times in the course of a year as you play during the course of a week. This is because strings lose their natural resilience and elasticity and begin to play dead, giving you no control over the ball. The more spin you put on the ball, the more likely you are to break strings. However, don't rush to change your most effective strokes in order to save cash! Instead, follow some simple tips, and get the most from your strings.

1. Don't subject strings to extremes of temperature, i.e. don't leave racquets unattended in the boot of your car. This can lead to brittleness.
2. Dry your strings with a cloth after playing in damp conditions.
3. Similarly brush off any loose particles after playing on a clay court. (Pay extra attention to the string holes.)
4. Make sure string protection strips and inserts (where strings meet the frame) are not split and cutting into strings.
5. Check that knots are ideally double, and not slipping through the string holes.
6. Do not allow strings to become very displaced. Ease them back into position between points. If it becomes a constant problem, you might consider using string protection grommets or tablets. These are placed where strings touch each other in the hitting zone of the racquet, and are available at most good sports retailers. Remember, it's the strings that hit the ball for you, not your racquet!

KIT CHECK

Many pros like to have their racquets strung a few pounds tighter when playing on faster surfaces or with lighter balls, and looser when playing on slower clay courts or with heavy balls.

KIT CHECK

Always try to have a minimum of two identical racquets when playing, in order to be prepared for a broken string during a match.

RULES CHECK

Your strings must consist of a pattern of crossed strings connected to a frame, and you are not allowed to add any additional stringing or object designed to impart additional spin to the ball.

Tennis Balls

At first glance, it seems the easiest thing in the world to walk into a shop (almost any shop!) and buy yourself some tennis balls, but be warned: many of these, if purchased, will perform with all the aerodynamic and flight characteristics of the average house brick. Price alone is no determinant of quality when it comes to tennis balls, but at least it's a starting point.

Those balls marked 'Championship' on sale at 50p each in your local post office, garage or corner shop may look tempting, but try hitting them on court and they will probably play more like golf balls or balls of wool. The major championships around the world rely on a few major manufacturers to provide them with quality tennis balls that match a stringent performance standard, as outlined in the ITF (International Tennis Federation) Rules of Tennis. These standards take account of such factors as air pressure and climatic conditions, for it would obviously be unrealistic to expect the same ball to perform equally well at both sea-level and 30,000 feet above. Size, weight, bounce, etc., are all regulated most carefully, so in this way, if you purchase a can of balls endorsed by the ITF or a national governing body, you know that you are getting a quality product.

Basically, your choice is between pressurized balls, sold in a can and packed under vacuum conditions (they give off a discernible hiss when opened), or pressure-less balls, sold in cans or boxes and often identified as Extra or Long Life.

For tournament play, pressurized balls are indisputably the best, but you must accept that as soon as they are opened they start to deteriorate (hence the regular ball changes as seen on TV during major tournaments). Pressure-less balls are good for practice and for consistent indoor surfaces (where they retain the same bounce for a long period), or for outdoor surfaces for a shorter period where, although they stay hard, they start to fly around like golf balls when they become abraded.

Do be honest with yourself when buying tennis balls. Pressurized are certainly the best for a tournament

Don't skimp on the quality of your balls.

match when they are brand new, but equally certainly, they are the worst for social tennis when they are a few weeks old. Tennis is a difficult enough game in itself without worrying about consistency in the bounce of the ball. Buy the right ball for your circumstances; it will benefit your game in the long term. Do throw out pressurized balls when they get too old. Remember, this does not necessarily mean when the outer covering is worn off them. A badly bouncing ball will do nothing to improve your tennis at all.

Increasingly, national coaching organizations are recognizing the benefits of learning tennis with softer, low compression balls that make maintaining a rally easier to master. In Britain, the LTA have a system of Mini Tennis Red (for children of eight and under), Mini Tennis Orange (ages eight and nine) and Mini Tennis Green (for ages nine and ten and above). Thus, children progress easily from the softest (red) ball all the way up to the adult (yellow) ball. Similarly, the ITF now recommends that adults being introduced to the game start with the green ball in order to get to grips with playing the game more quickly.

Clothing

If you're just starting in the game on a public court, you can play in whatever you are most comfortable, but clubs will sometimes insist on the 'predominantly white' rule. Although this seems superficially pretentious, it makes a lot of sense really, since white is certainly the coolest and therefore easiest colour to wear on a hot day. Style and fashion will determine your choice beyond this, but ensure that you buy loose-fitting garments with soft, non-abrasive seams. Tennis is a free-flowing game that requires total mobility at all times, so it makes sense not to strap yourself into a tight-fitting garment that will burst open on every wide-running backhand! Modern fibre technology has made a huge difference to player comfort. Where natural fabrics like cotton used to be a much better bet than synthetic fibres, today you can buy lightweight specialized materials that will either keep you warm in winter or will wick moisture away from your body in summer and thereby keep you cool.

A good warm-up suit is a worthwhile investment, and again, do not be too strapped by the dictates of fashion over and above function. Buy a suit that you can easily slip off over your tennis shoes, and loose enough to allow you to hit the ball freely. There is no reason on earth why you shouldn't play tennis through the winter months, protected against the extremes of cold by a well-designed tracksuit. Again, modern fibres ensure that you no longer have to endure tracksuits that get wetter and heavier the more you play. For real outdoor diehards, the type of gloves used by runners are perfect for protecting your hands from extreme cold and wind, without having to sacrifice the sensation of control over your grip on the racquet. Just add a baseball cap with a peak designed to keep the sun out of your eyes and you'll be good to go!

TOP TIP

'The logical and sensible dress for tennis is the one that gives you the greatest amount of freedom at all times.' Helen Wills, 1928 French Open, Wimbledon, US Open and Olympic champion.

KIT CHECK

If you are a two-handed player, make sure your clothing has got a pocket for the spare ball when you are serving. You don't want to be forced into playing a one-handed backhand just because you're holding a ball!

Tennis Shoes

Tennis shoes have come (thankfully) a long way from the simple canvas upper and rubber sole models of the grass court era, but making a selection of the right shoe today is about more than just considering whether the colour complements your on-court clothing or not! Biomechanical research has shown that a runner transmits a force of two to three times his own bodyweight through the foot to the ground, so it makes a great deal of sense today to consider adequate cushioning for the ball of the foot.

Moreover, the court surface will influence the choice of shoe it is wisest for you to purchase. Indoor carpet weave surfaces require a slick sole that will not abrade the surface or provide so much traction that you are in danger of blisters or turning an ankle. Grass courts have an inherent cushioning effect of their own, so you can get away with a thinner sole on this surface. The pros frequently use a difficult-to-obtain pimple sole for grass court play but unfortunately many clubs don't like their members using these as they can tear up the grass. All-weather hard courts require a greater degree of protection through the sole, and clay courts require a sole that allows you to slide into your shots, so a simple herringbone sole pattern is often the best. There is also a specialist type of sole that is best suited to playing on artificial grass (astroturf) courts, so there is literally a shoe for every eventuality. Fortunately, if you're just starting out, you won't go far wrong with a simple hard-court model.

To a certain extent, style of play should also be considered, as a baseliner will normally require more side shoe cushioning than a serve and volleyer, who needs more protection in the toe box and heel area. If you're already a competent player, in order to determine what shoes you should be buying, first thoroughly analyse an old pair and recognize where the shoes have broken down or worn out quickly. This will give you a guide to choosing the correct shoe for your needs that provides you with extra protection or strength in those particular areas. If you already suffer from a known foot injury, it's a good idea to visit one of the specialist sports shoe retailers who can assess your gait and the best shoe for your needs by a computer analysis of your running style carried out on the store's treadmill.

If you're new to the game, read the manufacturers' literature describing the shoes' design and characteristics. Choose a model with adequate cushioning for the surface you intend to play most on. Ensure the heel cup is a snug fit without being tight, and remember that your feet expand under the heat of a playing situation, so make sure you have room. (Ideally, wear two pairs of socks when trying models on). Above all, make sure the shoes you buy are comfortable. Many players choose a shoe size one up from their normal size in order to avoid their toes banging up against the front of the shoe when making sudden stop/start movements. Manufacturers are constantly improving their products and combining lightness with durability, comfort and technical developments.

Choose a shoe with adequate cushioning for the surface you intend to play on most often.

Some players favour choosing 'Hi-top' shoes, which come above the ankle and consequently provide stability for the ankle joint. These may be suitable for you if you have a problem in this area, but remember that extra support leads to extra weight and (generally speaking) you should go for as light a shoe as possible within the parameters you have set yourself on durability, comfort and protection.

'Cross-trainers' that incorporate the specific characteristics of shoes designed for different sports can be useful. You can now step off the tennis court onto a running track and attend the gym afterwards, without changing your footwear in between. These models are undoubtedly good for the recreational player, but if you're serious about your tennis you should buy specialized shoes. Indeed, many clubs will not allow cross-trainers, which may cause damage to court surfaces.

It is still, however, true that you get what you pay for, so think twice about the very cheap shoes often described as tennis shoes. The very real risk of an injury that might curtail your time on court makes thorough research prior to purchase a necessity.

KIT CHECK

If you intend to play tournaments, wear shoes designed for the surface you're playing on and avoid injury.

CHAPTER 3

PLAYING

Courts and Clubs

In Britain, there are a huge number of outdoor public tennis courts and many local councils are increasingly recognizing the importance of this community asset and upgrading them. In order to get a game, it is often sufficient to simply turn up and pay or, if you're lucky, play for free. Many popular facilities now utilize online or phone pre-booking systems, so it is worth checking this out in advance. There are also a large number of local authority-managed indoor courts where you can play at very reasonable cost.

The other access route to British tennis courts is via the club structure. This is no bad thing, as joining a club automatically puts you into contact with like-minded individuals, and thus raises the level of your game by the increase of knowledge you acquire both on and off the court.

The club scene in Britain may be broadly split into two rather distinct camps. On the one hand, there is the older established, rather traditional idea of a tennis club, often run by volunteers, and situated usually in residential areas. For this type of club, you should attend normally on a Saturday or Sunday, introduce yourself to a member of the committee, and hopefully play a few games. At this time, your playing standard may well be discreetly observed, and (depending on circumstances) you may be accepted, or placed on a waiting list.

On the other hand, there are the newer, often larger clubs, frequently situated away from residential areas, but with good transport links. Many of these are luxury complexes, complete with fully equipped gymnasia, restaurant facilities, swimming pools, etc. This type of club typically has indoor tennis facilities as its major attraction. Being professionally staffed and run, joining is often a simple

Visit several local tennis clubs before deciding which one is right for you.

A few lessons can be a good investment.

matter of picking up a leaflet and being able to afford the (often large) fees involved.

Whatever type of club you opt for, you should apply the same criteria when making your choice:

1. Is the club easily accessible to you? Your tennis will improve faster if you can make spur of the moment decisions to play, rather than having to continually plan in advance.
2. Does the court surface allow for year-round play? Clubs with clay courts only will be unplayable during frosty weather, while the grass court season seldom lasts more than four months.
3. Has the club the back-up facilities you require, i.e. adequate changing facilities if coming direct from work, or indeed a sauna if that is what you require?
4. Does the club have the right feel for you? You will improve quicker if you're happy with your environment.

Coaching

By now, you're well equipped to go out and conquer the tennis world, but you should consider taking a few lessons. Given that the world's top playing pros all employ coaches, there is a surprising resistance among better club players to enlist a coach for help with their game.

The point to remember is that no matter what an individual's playing standard may be (and this includes coaches as well) an external observer is always better placed to analyze the actual mechanics of a stroke as it is taking place. Therefore, the benefits of coaching should not be overlooked, even if it is merely an occasional check-up rather than a series of stroke improvement lessons.

In choosing a coach, look first for some level of qualification to teach tennis, and secondly, for someone you can get on with and therefore learn from more effectively. The LTA website outlines the various levels of coaching qualification currently recognized in the UK and it makes good sense to determine that your coach is committed to the highest standards of professionalism, client safety and ethical behaviour. Try to watch several working before deciding on your choice, as all coaches are individuals and one style or approach may suit you better than another.

Having made your choice, arrange plenty of practice sessions between your lessons. It makes no sense at all to walk onto a court only once every fortnight, and then only for a coaching lesson. Your money will be largely wasted and progress slow. Aim to practise what you have learned at least twice between lessons. Keep at it, and the extra small amount of effort will pay certain dividends.

It is also worthwhile considering the growing number of tennis holiday venues around the world that allow you to enjoy the holiday of your choice at the same time as receiving expert tuition. Total immersion in tennis for a period of up to a fortnight's holiday can do marvels for your game.

Tournaments

Sooner or later, everyone reaches a certain stage in their tennis development when they should consider entering a tournament. It is here that you can measure yourself against a variety of different players and put into effect what has been practised in a non-competitive situation. It is therefore a pity that too many players have in the past bypassed this essential stage of improving their game, believing themselves to be not up to tournament standard and perhaps embarrassed about the possibility of losing badly in the first round. Thankfully, however, this need no longer be the case, as an increasing number of tournaments are now available nationally, based on the 'rating system'.

At club level, players will be assessed as being at a particular standard or rating. Tournaments are then organized in such a way that you compete with others of a similar standard. As your wins increase, so your rating rises and the level of competition you experience goes up accordingly.

Juniors have a similar system in Britain via the Mini Tennis scheme, where youngsters start at Mini Red, then progress through to Mini Orange and Mini Green before starting to play with the yellow ball in age groups up to the under-eighteen category. Beyond eighteen, players compete in open age group competition, although at age thirty-five you may decide that playing against those tough eighteen-year-olds has become a little difficult for you. At this stage you may, if you wish, opt to play in the seniors category, which has opportunities to play in the over-thirty-fives, forties, etc., up to the over-eighty-fives!

All such events are fully computerized, so it is easy to keep track of how your game is improving and maybe check on your GB ranking on the LTA website or world ranking on the ITF website.

TOP TIP

'You can do anything that you want in your lifetime. Everybody can. All you have to do is believe in it and work hard enough to get it. You're not born into any position – that's not the way it works.' Ivan Lendl, Australian, French and US Open Champion and coach to Andy Murray (*Tennis 93*, 1990).

Sponsorship

For the improving junior player, sponsorship is a useful way of reducing the costs of tennis. Most manufacturing companies incorporate a sponsorship or 'terms' programme into their promotional budget, and they are often on the lookout for more promising young players who will use their equipment and be seen by others to be using it.

Obviously, all firms hope to see their contracted players rise to the top, when the widespread publicity the player receives will have a spin-off effect on the equipment he or she is using. The top pros today often earn far more from their endorsement contracts than they do from tournament winnings.

With a few wins under his belt, the promising junior looking for sponsorship should make a list of firms whose equipment they like (addresses are easily obtainable through the internet), and then write to, email or phone the company's Promotions Department, asking for a 'terms application form'. This form will typically ask you to state your best recent results, tennis history, planned coming tournaments, etc., and may ask for a recent photo of you in playing gear. You will then be notified as to whether you are to be accepted as a terms player and, if this is the case, a contract specifying the terms of the agreement will be forwarded for signature by yourself, or by your parents if you are under eighteen.

Do remember, though, that sponsorship is designed to work both ways, and you should obviously give your best endeavours to promoting the company's products in a positive way at all times. In this way, you will develop a relationship that will equally benefit your sponsor and your own tennis development.

Etiquette

A knowledge of court etiquette or accepted standards of behaviour can add hugely to one's enjoyment of tennis but, surprisingly, not much of this appears in writing anywhere. In the UK, the LTA have a Fair Play code of conduct which asks young players in their FutureStars programme to:

- Try their hardest in matches and practice
- Give a good impression of themselves and British Tennis
- Be a good sport by showing fair play and respecting the rules
- Show respect to other people

- Wear the Aegon (sponsor's) FutureStars patch.

There is a similar code of conduct for parents and guardians to sign up to as well.

Mostly, it seems that through playing for years, tennis players have reached a sort of collective understanding as to those little things that, together, ensure that concentration remains fixed on the task in hand and not on any arbitrary distractions that may occur. Some of the following suggestions might therefore be helpful if you are new to tennis, or not playing with an umpire present.

1. Familiarize yourself with the rules of tennis.
2. Realize that it is your obligation to make all the calls regarding what is happening on your side of the net, just as it is your opponent's responsibility to make the calls on his side. Therefore, start every match from a position of trusting your opponent.
3. If you have any doubts at all as to whether a ball on your side of the net was good or not, give your opponent the benefit of the doubt and play the ball as good. Don't ask for a let. Remember, what happens on your side of the net is your responsibility. You should, of course, help your opponent in making a call when he or she asks you to.
4. Make all your calls instantaneously and don't ask spectators whether they thought the ball was in or not, or you will soon find yourself involved in distracting arguments. Similarly, if you do call a ball out accidentally and then realize your mistake, correct the call immediately.
5. When you're serving, try to announce the score regularly, so that the opportunity for disagreement is minimized. If you do find yourself completely unable to agree on the score, however, the best thing to do is to go back to the last point when you were in agreement and continue from that point. Alternatively, you could consider spinning a racquet.
6. Don't stall, intentionally distract your opponent, swear or throw your racquet about. You may feel you're releasing tension, but you're probably putting even more pressure on yourself, as well as revealing your mental state to your opponent and looking an idiot.
7. Remember if you're playing in a tournament that coaching from the sidelines is forbidden under ITF rules.
8. A much ignored point of etiquette on English public courts is that you should, as a simple matter of courtesy to others, wait until a point is over before walking behind a court where a game is in progress. It is often the case that a ball from your court has rolled over behind your neighbour's court. Wait politely until their play has ceased before either going to get it or asking for it to be returned. Of course, if your ball is rolling dangerously towards them and they haven't spotted it, let them know immediately in order to avoid their becoming injured. Similarly, return your neighbours' balls promptly. (Public courts often appear to be similar to black holes in space. Balls go onto them obviously enough in cans of three or four, but mysteriously come off only in ones or twos!)
9. Feed the ball to your opponent in the warm-up before a match, and don't use the situation to either practise your passing shots or try and blast the ball at 100mph. Don't bother returning all of your opponent's warm-up serves. Instead, collect the balls and serve them all back again.
10. Try and abide by local dress/footwear rules. For instance, some clubs insist on a certain type of sole on your tennis shoe in order to minimize the risk of court damage. Similarly, many clubs have a tradition of predominantly white clothing (which actually makes sound sense, as it is often the coolest alternative, and does not show up unsightly sweat marks).
11. At the end of a match, shake your opponent's hand and (if you have won) offer to buy him a drink. It is a small price to pay for having managed to succeed in your immediate short-term objective of winning, and it should go a long way to ensuring you are never short of competitive practice partners!

What Are You Good At and What Could You Be Better At?

A business, when setting corporate objectives and strategies, will not make a move until it has completed a positive evaluation of where it sits at the present moment, taking into account its own strengths and weaknesses, and measuring those against the available opportunities and threats. Similarly, you should do a SWOT analysis (Strengths, Weaknesses, Opportunities, Threats) on yourself and your own game. What are your particular strengths? Is it your forehand? Your powerful serve? Your will to win? Your ability to run every shot down?

Strengths	Weaknesses
Opportunities	Threats

A SWOT analysis sheet.

Where is your game most vulnerable? Are you nervous of your backhand? Does the thought of approaching the net worry you? What are the opportunities available to you in tennis? Would joining a club enable you to meet more people? Would your level of health and fitness improve

Stay focused on both your short- and long-term goals.

radically? And what are the obstacles or threats standing in the way of your development? Have you only a limited amount of time in which to practise, or do you live miles away from the nearest court? Draw up a SWOT analysis of your game to give yourself a starting point for improvement and development. Identification of problems is the first step in eradicating them!

When looking at your game in detail, list out all your groundstrokes, your serves, your net game (that's forehand and backhand, high and low volleys, wide on both sides, and your overhead smash on both sides), your speed around the court, your level of concentration, perseverance, etc. Next, grade these on a sliding scale of 0 to 10, and then ask a friend who has played you many times to do the same. In this way, you should develop a picture of where your strengths and weaknesses lie, and give yourself a starting point from which to begin a real improvement in your game. All players, including those at the very top, recognize that they have weaknesses, and strive consciously to minimize these and improve their strengths at all times.

Having identified your most common mistakes, you will be in a position to do something about them. At this stage, it is as well to remember that the single most important aspect of any tennis stroke (and therefore the point you should pay closest attention to) is the impact point or moment of contact between the ball and the racquet face. You can get away with all sorts of weird and wonderful beginnings and endings to all the strokes of tennis, but you can get away with virtually nothing if your racquet face is not almost vertical at the moment it makes contact with the ball. (Even the spin shots require a racquet face that is considerably closer to vertical than it actually feels.)

Basically, the ball goes wherever your racquet directs it. If you're hitting long, the face is probably tilted back (or open to the sky) too much. If you're hitting in the net, the face is probably tilted down (or closed) too much.

Having become aware of what your racquet face is doing, experiment with correcting it and always exaggerate your corrections. If you've identified a lot of balls going short into the net, don't try and hit net-skimmers all the time; instead, try to hit every stroke two metres over the top of the net until you get a real feeling for the stroke and for the distance and placement involved.

Finally, remember, you can only improve your game if you work hard at practice, and this doesn't mean playing points all the time. Find someone who also wants to improve, and help each other. There is just as much enjoyment and reward involved in a concentrated, effective practice session as there is in any number of games played purely for points, and anyway, the real rewards will become quickly apparent when those strokes that you thought of as weaknesses quickly become seen as strengths by your opponents!

KEY POINTS

1. Be aware of your own strengths and weaknesses.
2. Actively try to minimize your weaknesses and maximize your strengths.
3. Use the warm-up time to analyze your opponent's strengths and weaknesses.
4. Be prepared to take time out between tournaments in order to work on improving your game.
5. Practise regularly.

TOP TIP

'All the time, you hope for a clean, crisp stroke and that comes only if you are prepared to hit literally hundreds of shots, most days of the week.' Steffi Graf (Durham, Andy, *Play to Win*, Octopus, 1987).

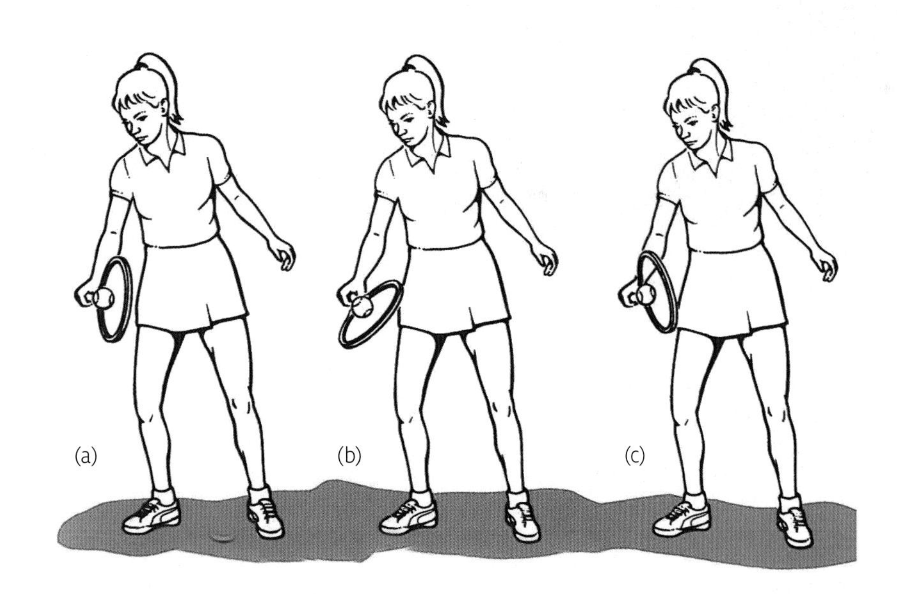

If the basic lifted swing is attempted, the angle of the racquet face in (a) will ensure a good shot while that in (b) will send the ball long,and (c) will put the ball into the net.

PART 2

SKILLS AND TECHNIQUES

CHAPTER 4

RACQUET CONTROL AND GRIP

Control

Good tennis begins and ends with racquet control and the absolute certainty that a player carries into each stroke, knowing the precise angle of alignment necessary between the racquet face and the ball in order to achieve the planned and desired result. In short, 'You gotta know what your racquet's doing!'

For groundstrokes, you should aim to swing the racquet at the ball. The stroke is not a push or a short stab. The feeling you are trying to attain is that of a swing that allows the racquet to move smoothly to and through the ball under its own weight and volition. Obviously, timing here is critical, and this will only come with practice and experience, but the closer you can get to letting the racquet do the work for you, the better your tennis will become. Imagine that you are going to throw the racquet away from you with an underhand movement and you will start to understand the freedom that your groundstrokes should experience.

For serving, try to get the feel of throwing your racquet. Just as you would throw a cricket or tennis ball a long distance, so should you feel that you could, if you wished, release your racquet during the serving motion and see it fly away from you both upwards and outwards. This movement is not completely natural for some people, and it is worth practising. Simply stand behind the baseline in a side-on stance and practise throwing the ball first high over the net, then further into the stop netting and then over the stop netting and out of the court. Be aware as you are doing this of the linkage between the various body

The serve flows upwards through the body, from the toes through to the wrist and racquet head.

parts that contribute to a more powerful throw. Power will come from the legs and ankles, up through the trunk and out through the shoulder, elbow, hand and wrist.

Consequently, when you serve, visualize a throwing movement and keep your elbow high, while relaxing your wrist and allowing the racquet to drop down behind your shoulder. Then explode the movement upwards and outwards using the wrist, elbow and shoulder to generate speed through the racquet head.

For volleying, the standard advice is to punch the racquet head forwards at the ball. Be sure, though, not to punch excessively from the shoulder. The movement comes very much from a short explosive forwards movement of the elbow, and might perhaps be more accurately described as a short karate-style chopping movement, as if you were chopping with the underside edge of the hand.

The range of movement in this stroke is very slight, and the racquet will probably travel only 30–50cm in a forward direction, so don't be tempted to make it any bigger or you will lose the shot's effectiveness.

Remember: control your swing, your throw and your punch for effective racquet technique.

Allied to racquet head control must be racquet face control. At the precise moment of impact between the ball and the racquet face, you should be aware of the angle produced between your strings and the ball itself. For most strokes, the angle should be nearly straight on or 90 degrees to the horizontal. For some strokes this varies slightly, as in topspin where the angle may vary towards 70 degrees, with the racquet face directed slightly more towards the court.

For all variations on flat strokes, the angle will change slightly, but the measurement of that angle is not important. It is not the place of this book to say that such and such a precise angle of inclination is correct or not, for when it comes down to where it matters, on the court, how on earth can you do anything about it? What is important is to realize constantly that the ball will only go in the direction that you hit it. Therefore, you should seek to develop a thorough understanding, through practice, of how to hit the full range of spin shots as well as normal flat or lifted drives, serves and volleys, etc. In this way, you will make yourself more aware of the minute adjustments that are necessary in order to radically affect the flight of the ball in a given direction.

Remember, focus on your racquet face at impact point, and gain control over your placements.

RULES CHECK

Sometimes, you may see the pros throw their racquet at a ball when they are caught out of position. It always gets a laugh from the crowd but, unfortunately, even if it produces a successful hit, the point is lost. The rules state that the racquet must be held in the hand when the stroke is made.

The full Western grip allows for heavy topspin on the ball.

Grip

First, let's get one thing straight. This section is not intended to make you think that there is only one way of holding the racquet for a particular stroke and that everything else is wrong. We all have things that work for us as individuals, and therefore you should carry on doing what you're good at, and merely experiment with a view towards adding variety to your game.

Hopefully, tennis coaching has moved on from the experience I had as a good county level junior. When I started to achieve some tournament success, I was awarded subsidized coaching at the hands of a professional. Unfortunately, this gentleman had very definite views about what constituted a correct forehand, and worked systematically to remove my somewhat unorthodox (for those days) topspin forehand, thereby completely missing the point that it was this very stroke that was responsible for my being with him in the first place!

The message is clear. Play up to your strengths and seek to minimize your weaknesses. This section, therefore, is merely a guide to what you might achieve with certain forms of grip. Some of the grips you may have heard described are the Continental, the Eastern, the Semi-Western, the Western, the Eastern backhand and the Extreme Eastern or Semi-Western backhand.

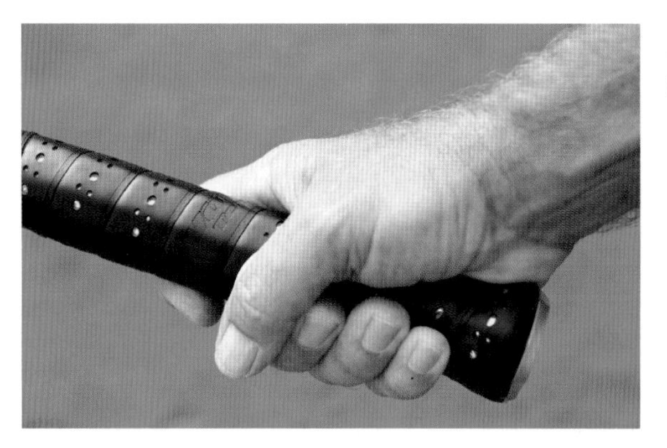

Eastern forehand with the palm behind the handle.

The Continental Grip

This is also called the Chopper or Service grip. It is an extremely versatile grip and is used primarily for serves, volleys, overheads, slices and defensive shots. Place your hand on the top of the handle so that the V between your thumb and first finger is aligned with the top of the handle. It should make you feel that you can chop against something with the edge of the racquet, much as you would use an axe to chop a piece of wood. Visualize yourself hitting a nail with the edge of your racquet frame, and you have got this grip. Better still, practise bouncing a ball on the edge, up and down on the court, and you should have naturally assumed the Continental.

Obviously, as a compromise, you can expect to be able to hit both forehands and backhands adequately with this grip, but it lacks both the ability to hit with strength on the backhand, and with consistent powerful topspin on the forehand.

The grip is ideally suited for the type of low bounce found on grass courts, and of course it is ideal for volleying, where you often do not have the time to react quickly enough with a grip change between forehand and backhand. In using this grip for volleys, you will find that you are naturally achieving a certain amount of backspin on the ball, but this is no bad thing, as spin equals control in most cases.

Ideally suited for the service, the Chopper grip provides you with the alternatives of hitting either a flat, sliced or topspin delivery, which is why it is sometimes referred to as the Service grip (although again, there is room for confusion here as many people prefer to serve with a grip that is much more towards the backhand position).

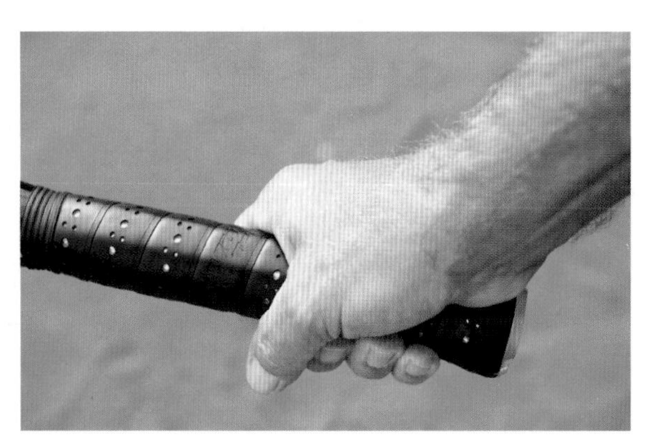

The Continental is an extremely versatile grip.

The Eastern Forehand Grip

This grip is exactly the same as the position you would place your palm in, if you were to try and step towards the ball and strike it dead centre in the middle of the palm of your hand. In other words, it is a grip that allows the racquet to become an extension of your arm.

To find this grip, hold the racquet with your non-playing hand, out in front of you on edge, with the butt end pointing towards you. Now place your playing hand flat against the strings, and draw it down towards the handle. You should feel just as if you were shaking hands with the racquet.

You can check that you have got the right grip by running the index finger of your left hand down the top right-hand edge of the racquet, all the way to your playing hand. You should finish up in the V formed between your racquet-hand thumb and index finger.

This grip will provide you with a lot of stability on forehand ground strokes and volleys, and allows for both limited topspin and slice, but it does not give enough versatility for the serve. It's easy to switch quickly to other grips from the Eastern, making it a good choice for players who like to come to the net. On the downside, it's hard to deal with high balls to the forehand and it tends to produce flatter strokes that may lack consistency.

The Semi-Western Grip

This grip supposedly came out of the west coast of America, where slower clay courts with their characteristically higher bounce led players naturally into a style of play that relied heavily on staying at the baseline and winning from there, without any real need to come to the net and volley. As a result, what was needed was a stroke that had plenty of net clearance for safety, yet pinned one's opponent back, and at the same time kicked high in the air to make their return even harder. Thus was topspin invented, and with it the Western forehand grip.

The full Western forehand allows for heavy topspin on the ball.

As topspin relies on hitting up the back of the ball in a low to high movement, the standard Eastern grip gets too much behind the ball and results in a high flyer that has no spin. What is needed is a grip that allows the racquet face to brush up the back of the ball naturally, and the Western grip provides this.

To find this grip, simply put your racquet down on the court and then pick it up again. Don't adjust your grip in any way. You will find that you picked it up quite naturally with your palm behind the handle of the racquet, and this is the way you should hold it to strike your shot. Many children come to topspin a great deal more naturally than adults who try to develop the stroke in later years, simply because this is the way a child picks up a racquet, so therefore this is the way he plays with it.

It's a great grip for taking a big swing, as the topspin imparted will help keep the ball in court. At the same time, it's good for driving flat winners as the strike zone is further out in front of the body than the Eastern forehand.

The problem with the Semi-Western is that it makes low bouncing balls very difficult to control, and balls hit straight at the body have to be 'shovelled' back. It gives no control on the forehand volley, and for serving it is much too limiting, as you can only hit a hard flat delivery with no choice about hitting varieties of spin. Also, the degree of grip change required between hitting a forehand and hitting a backhand is huge and, on fast courts, it is obviously better to have as little going on between the strokes as possible in terms of adjustments that may happen too late and put you under unnecessary pressures.

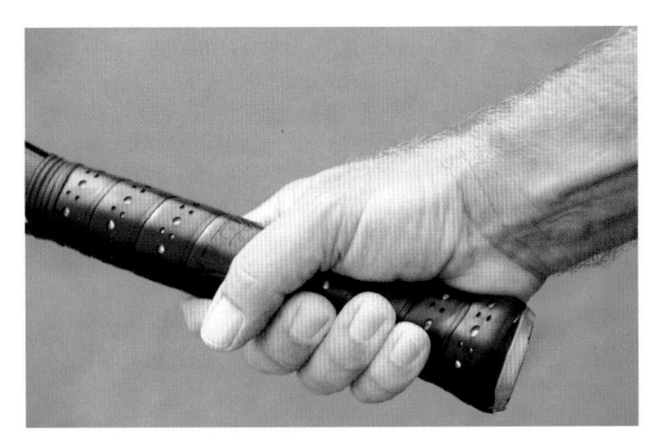

The semi-Western forehand.

The Western Grip

From a Semi-Western grip, shift your knuckle one more bevel clockwise and you've got a full Western grip. Looking down at the racquet, your knuckle should be on the very bottom of the grip. Your palm will be almost completely under the racquet. This is a good grip for clay court players and those who hit with heavy topspin. As an extreme grip, producing topspin is made easier. Also, because the strike zone is higher and further out in front, it is good for handling high bouncing balls. On the downside, low bouncing balls are extremely difficult to play with this grip, which is why players who favour it tend to be clay court specialists who may struggle on faster surfaces. It also demands a lot of physical strength.

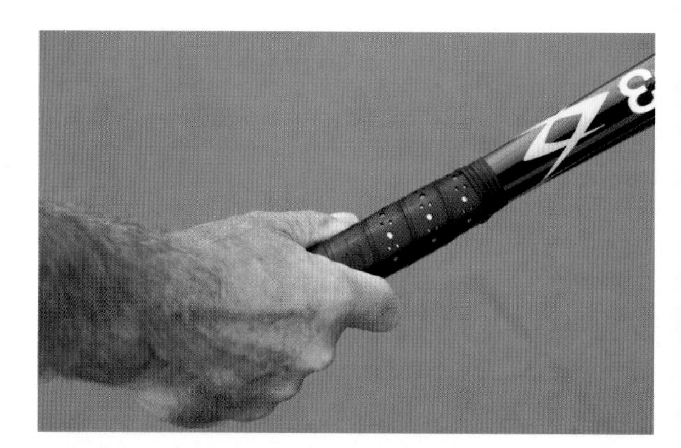

The Eastern backhand.

The Eastern Backhand Grip

The standard Eastern backhand grip is achieved by starting from the Continental position, and then rotating the grip a quarter turn to the left (for right-handers). If you run your left-hand index finger down the left-hand edge of your racquet, you should find that you finish up in the V formed between your racquet hand index finger and thumb. For many players, this position does not feel firm enough on the racquet, so you may wish to try pushing your thumb up the handle behind the racquet face in order to give extra support.

The whole point of this backhand grip is to achieve a solid racquet face at impact point, as the stroke is inherently a weaker one than the forehand. This is because the palm is no longer behind the racquet at impact, and hence no longer gives support and stability.

Keep your hands close together on the two-handed backhand.

Another way to find the correct position of the grip is to simply swing the back of your hand as if you were going to hit a ball with it, and stop at the precise moment at which you would be achieving contact. At this point, the back of your hand should be perpendicular to the ground and directly over your front foot. Now simply place your racquet into this grip, so that it too is perpendicular to the court. Again, you should feel that the racquet is merely an extension of your arm.

This grip will provide you with the ability to hit most backhand shots satisfactorily, but you may care to experiment by moving slightly more towards the forehand in order to hit with slice, and back in a more exaggerated fashion to hit heavy topspin backhands. It's also good for hitting kick serves and preparing for the volley. The downside is that high bouncing balls to the backhand are very difficult to deal with and you will often be forced to rely on a defensive slice in order to deal with these.

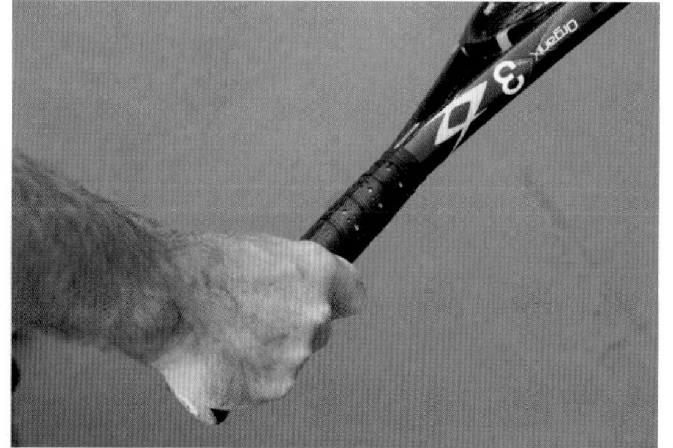

The extreme Eastern or semi-Western backhand.

Extreme Eastern, or Semi-Western Backhand Grip

This is the equivalent of the Western forehand. The base knuckle of your index finger should move round anti-clockwise one bevel from the Eastern backhand. It requires a certain amount of strength, but has the benefit of both producing heavy topspin and allowing higher bouncing balls to be struck more firmly, thus making it a bit of a specialist shot used mainly by clay court players.

The Two-Handed Grip

This is not really very different from any of the previously mentioned grips, other than the placement of the additional hand as close as you can get it to the lower hand. The dominant hand is usually placed in the Continental grip, with the non-dominant hand in the Semi-Western forehand.

It's a great choice for youngsters starting out in tennis, who often need the extra stability afforded by two hands in order to overcome any problems caused by inherently weaker wrists. Double-handed players hit with a great deal of strength normally but are limited in their reach on the ball, and therefore have to run further and be fitter in order to arrive at a balanced position from which to achieve contact on the stroke.

One of the benefits of the two-handed approach is that control of the racquet face can be gained by the use of the top hand turning the wrist while at the same time stabilizing it. Thus, two-handers can often hit both forehands and backhands with only the minimum of grip change on the part of their lower hand. For one-handers, this is not possible because of the previously stated inherent weakness in the backhand stroke.

If you tend to take a clenched fist-type grip to your shots, you might try to spread the fingers a little. Many players bunch their fingers together, and in so doing lose a degree of control over the racquet. The more feel you can get on your racquet handle the better, but if this seems totally unnatural to you – like any of the other advice I have given here – ignore it!

Tennis is a game for individuals, and you should never interfere with something that comes totally naturally to you and provides good results. Take advice by all means and experiment as much as you like, but at the end of the day it's down to you to develop your own style of play that is best suited to your own individual requirements.

KIT CHECK

Always carry some spare overwrap grips in your bag, especially on hot summer days.

CHAPTER 5

FOOTWORK AND BALANCE

One of the most vital keys to good tennis is the ability to hit the ball from any part of the court while in a balanced position. If you watch the pros play, you will notice just how easy they make the game look. This ease of stroke-making comes not just from their skill in executing the stroke itself, but also from the speed with which they have interpreted all the data available to them regarding where they needed to be on the

Both players are alert and in a balanced ready position.

The player has her weight on her toes, ready to move forward into the shot.

court in order to hit the next ball from a balanced position. In other words, they read the signs early, then moved efficiently into position. Thus, the starting point for good balance is efficient footwork.

Footwork

Nick Bollettieri, the American coach famous for producing a string of World No. 1 players, defines good footwork as being 'the ability to change direction quickly and smoothly with no wasted upper body movement'.

Take a look at today's top players. Without exception, they are all examples of supreme physical fitness, and this is obviously the starting point for efficient movement. Beyond this, they all take many small steps rather than a few larger ones, and they are never to be seen on their heels.

In order to move efficiently, you should be up on the balls of your feet all the time, ready to move left or right, forwards or backwards. A slightly 'pigeon-toed' stance is useful here, as this enables you to get off to a quick start by pushing off the inside of the foot, and driving hard to left or right. This up-on-the-toes positioning will enable you to step forward into the ball before impact, and consequently get maximum power and control. However, you should try to delay fully committing yourself onto the front foot for as long as possible, in case you find yourself stranded by a bad bounce or mistaken anticipation. Work instead to step forwards onto the heel of your leading foot, and then allow the delivery of the stroke itself to shift your weight forwards.

You should practise your movement around the court and take it as seriously as an athlete who measures his approach work carefully to the point of execution. High-jumpers and long-jumpers, for example, are skilled at judging how to arrive at the exact position with their lead leg, in order to get maximum benefit from their position relative to the take-off board. In the same way, you should become skilled at arriving at precisely the right point from which to play a balanced forehand or backhand.

One useful tip here would be to practise your approach from the mid-court to the net, without breaking your stride or introducing a hitch anywhere. This can be achieved by playing the forehand approach off the right foot (as a right-handed player), or by utilizing the carioca step on the backhand approach. This movement simply involves playing the backhand while allowing the trailing foot to come through from behind and overtake the leading foot. In this way, there is no need to pause on the approach, and your forward momentum can be maintained.

Balance

Good balance is the effective control of your centre of gravity, relative to the direction in which you are delivering the ball. If your balance is correct, dramatic passing shots hit on the run become possible, followed by quick recovery while still in a balanced position. This simple concept allows for a fantastic array of shots hit from impossible-looking positions. Top players like Novak Djokovic can play full-blooded drives from a full splits position, or with his back towards the net – shots which were never seen in the past. It all begins with the ready position. Knees should be flexed comfortably, the racquet pointing towards your opponent, weight on the balls of the feet, and the body bent slightly forwards at the waist. You should feel your centre of gravity located down through your hips.

In the same way, when running for a shot try to keep your centre of gravity under control. Run in an upright (or at the most, a slightly leaning) position, so that your balance point stays located in the hips. Many players make the mistake of leaning from the waist, which limits the stroke you can make and puts too much strain on your upper body and lower back muscles. Instead, take an extra step nearer to the ball if necessary, and get down low by using the legs and knees rather than the waist.

An excellent method I once saw a coach use to stop a player bending at the waist was to make him wear two hats on his head at the same time. Every time he bent at the waist, one hat fell off and he was penalized a point. This quickly reinforced the message and the player adjusted his stance. However, I appreciate you may not feel like doing this on a public court!

For balance on the service, keep your ball toss arm up in the air after release for as long as possible, and work on placing the ball out in front of your body, so that you can effectively transfer your weight through the ball at the precise moment of impact.

To practise maintaining good balance, work on drills like running through hoops or a training ladder at speed. This emphasizes rapid foot placement, coupled with the need to keep your head still and your balance point located within your body rather than outside your hips.

Also, you can practise drills like transferring a pile of tennis balls from one side of your body to a pace or two away on the other side, with only one ball in your hand at a time. If you put a stopwatch on this, or try and race a partner, you will quickly realize that the most efficient way to do it is to get down low using your knees rather than your waist. You will also find this a good aid to stamina if you really work at it.

Another excellent drill is the Hexagon, often used as a balance and agility test for assessing junior

Sequence of transferring balls one at a time from racquet to racquet is an ideal drill for both balance and stamina.

Sequence of transferring balls (continued).

performance players. A hexagon is chalked on the court with each side being two feet long and the angles between sides being 120 degrees. The player stands with both feet together in the centre of the hexagon, then, on the command of 'go', jumps with the feet still together out of the hexagon, then back again over the same line, and progressing through all six sides of the hexagon. The player is timed going through three complete cycles in a clockwise direction, then in an anti-clockwise direction. As one's times improve, so does one's balance and agility.

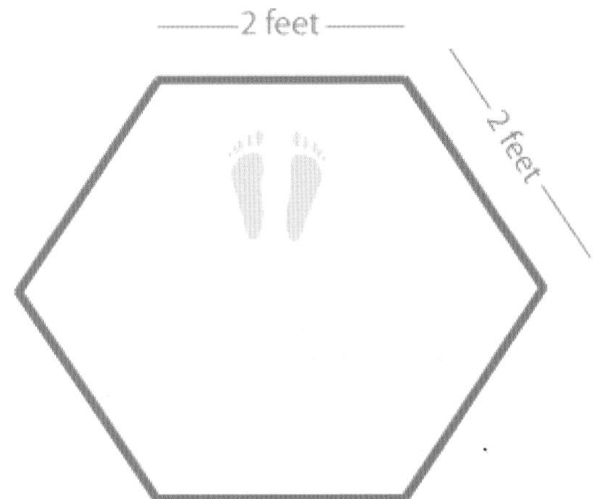

Hexagon balance/agility test.

CHAPTER 6

INDIVIDUAL SHOTS

The Forehand

People talk about the modern forehand, the classic forehand, the sliced forehand, etc., but they all have several stages in common, namely:

- The preparation
- The forward swing
- The impact point
- The follow through

The forehand is usually the first stroke adopted by someone beginning in tennis, and a lot has been said, written, discussed and disputed over the years regarding which grip it is best to adopt. For this reason, the best possible advice is to play with whatever you feel comfortable and you probably won't go very far wrong. If you are an older player and have played the game to some extent already, you might currently be playing with a Continental grip and a somewhat classical style of forehand. On the other hand, if you are a junior just starting out in tennis, you might have watched your favourite players on TV and found yourself copying their Western grips and harder-hitting modern forehand technique.

No matter what type of forehand you are hitting, your preparation should be early enough and timed against the speed of the oncoming ball to enable you to make a smooth transition into the forward swing that strikes the ball at the optimum point for achieving your intentions. The follow-through exists to remind you of the importance of your racquet face's angle at the moment of impact, and to allow the shot to naturally wind down ready for the next one.

Everything said so far can equally be applied to the backhand. We may now consider the four main varieties of forehand available. These are:-

- The flat/lifted (or classic) forehand
- The basic topspin forehand
- The modern forehand
- The sliced forehand

The racquet arm should swing freely through the shoulder and upper body.

The Flat/Lifted (or Classic) Forehand

Normally played with a Continental or Eastern grip, this classic stroke can be prepared for with either a straight take-back of the racquet or a looped take-back. Either way, the shoulders are turned in order to provide the optimum position for a free-flowing swing. The hips turn partially away from the net, and weight is transferred onto the front foot going forwards into the court. The swing should now occur comfortably from the shoulder in a rising stroke that comes from just below the height of the ball and finishes at around head height, the ball having been struck at a position just in front of the body and at around hip height. The follow-through will continue up and over the non-playing shoulder.

The general feeling you should get from this stroke can be compared with standing as a member of a human 'fire-chain', passing a fire-bucket from one person to another. You are more or less sideways, and transferring your body weight towards the net with a rotation of the trunk and upper torso. The result should be a smooth-flowing, relatively flat shot that you are aiming to hit close to your opponent's baseline.

(a) The shoulders have turned early and the racquet is taken well back.

(b) The racquet drops below the height of the oncoming ball.

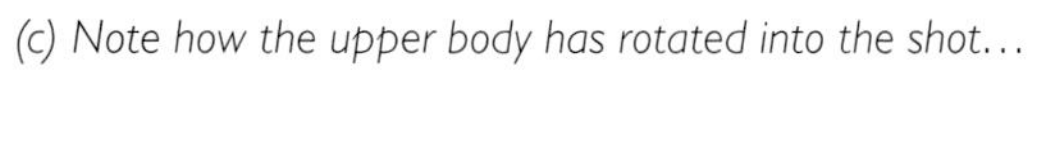

(c) Note how the upper body has rotated into the shot…

(d) …in a smooth low to high follow-through.

(e) The end result is a fluid stroke that utilizes the whole body weight and doesn't rely purely on the arm alone.

The Basic Topspin Forehand

Sometimes hit with an Eastern grip, but more often with a semi-Western, this shot gives an increased margin for error with its height over the net, depth, and high-kicking bounce. You can afford a more open stance towards the net if you like, but the real secret of hitting this shot lies not in body position, but in the angle of the racquet face as it brushes violently up the back of the ball at the impact point. Prepare by dropping your racquet face well below the oncoming ball, brush up the back and finish with a high follow-through. At the moment of impact, the racquet face should be almost vertical, and the result should be a high looped ball that carries with spin, pace and depth high over the net into your opponent's court.

This stroke is excellent for use on slow courts as it pins your opponent back, while with only marginal adjustment it can be used to great effect as a passing shot that dips away from the volleyer. Remember, however, that you cannot get effective topspin from a low bouncing ball, so ensure your footwork is quick enough to get you into the correct position from which to strike.

(a) Shoulders turn.

(b) Weight transfers onto the front foot.

(c) Racquet drops below height of oncoming ball.

(d) The stroke brushes up the back of the ball.

(e) The upper body rotates naturally…

(f) …and the power of the stroke produces a full follow-through.

The Modern Forehand

Played with a semi-Western or Western grip, the intention of this shot is to hit an aggressive and high-kicking ball that has a lot of work on it and is very difficult to return. It starts with a shoulder turn that goes back to the point at which the hips lock. The stance is relatively open with the weight loaded onto the right foot (for right-handers) and the foot itself turned slightly outwards. As the hips and shoulders start to open and uncoil, you should push off the right foot for additional power.

It is important to recognize that the power of this shot comes very much from the pivot and the shoulder turn. As the racquet comes forward, it trails slightly behind the wrist, snapping into contact with the ball as the hips turn fully to the front and the weight is transferred to the outside foot.

The shape of the stroke is very much low to high and the follow-through pulls up and across the body. Depending on the intention of the shot, the follow-through may take something of a windscreen wiper shape (for a lower trajectory but still aggressive bounce) or may even follow-through above the player's head in what looks almost like a lasso movement. Rafael Nadal developed this version of the swing in his years of growing up on heavy European clay. The result upon the ball in flight is almost to turn it egg-shaped in the air until it explodes off the opponent's court with a massive bounce. Television commentators have been heard to say that any shot received off Nadal's forehand has to be characterized as a forced error, so difficult is it for opponents to make an aggressive return from it.

(a–f) In this sequence, the wrist snap is clearly visible, adding to the power produced by the upward strike on the ball.

C

D

E

F

The Sliced Forehand

This stroke is to some extent out of favour in the modern style of aggressive baseline tennis and is most often seen as a defensive shot played when run out of position. However, it can produce an unexpected change of rhythm and pace that is good for forcing a steady opponent to adapt and change what they are doing.

To play this stroke, prepare by taking your racquet back higher than usual with an open-to-the-sky face and a Continental grip. You should aim to brush the open face down the underside of the ball in a long, high to low movement that contacts the ball in front of your body and also finishes well out in front.

If your first experiments with this shot result in a very high spinning ball, you are probably not getting enough high to low trajectory in your racquet path, so practise this until you can get a smooth floating ball that carries deep into your opponent's court and stays skidding low on impact. (Sliced balls make excellent approach shots, due to their low bounce and time-giving properties.)

> KEY POINT
>
> Sliced and topspin groundstrokes by definition entail a huge amount of energy being dissipated around the side of the ball rather than through it. Therefore, be positive and hit these shots hard in order to obtain maximum effect..

(a–c) The racquet is taken back high and cuts down the back of the ball in a high to low movement.

(d–f) The player recovers fully into the ready position.

> **TOP TIP**
>
> 'When I was very young and hanging around my parents' club in Czechoslovakia, I spent many an afternoon at the back wall, just banging groundstrokes against it, time after time after time. Not the most exciting memory perhaps, but those days formed the foundation of my groundstrokes.' Ivan Lendl, Australian, French and US Open Champion and coach to Andy Murray (*Hitting Hot*, Planet Books, 1987).

The Backhand

Single-handed or double-handed? There is no question that the predominant form of backhand drive today is the double-hander. The game has changed radically since the 1980s, with lighter racquets, a more physical and demanding style of play, an emphasis on winning from the back of the court, and yet – the player nicknamed the GOAT (Greatest Of All Time), Roger Federer, did it all with a single-handed backhand. So, where do we start?

Very young children new to the game will invariably find learning the double-hander easier. It stabilizes weak wrists, is less demanding on precision footwork and is good for developing early consistency. On the other hand, some children will wish to play in the style of the heroes they have watched on TV and will not experience problems in playing single-handed. As an older player wishing to improve your game, experiment and discover for yourself which approach feels more natural and comfortable for you.

The single-handed backhand allows for an easy transition to the net and a secure feeling on the backhand volley. If you play on faster courts (like grass) this could be a good option. The stroke also allows for an effective sliced backhand, which is not possible with two hands on the racquet.

The double-handed backhand is good for returning heavy serves and higher bouncing balls (more likely to be found on clay courts) and allows for greater consistency of shot-making through the enhanced stability of the racquet head. It also makes it easier to disguise the direction of a shot.

Experiment with both and make your choice!

The Double-Handed Backhand

This stroke commonly uses the Continental grip on the dominant hand and the Eastern on the non-dominant hand. In preparing for the shot, a split-step is taken to assist balance and positioning, and at the same time the hands come close together on the racquet handle. The shoulders and racquet turn together into the slot position, with the shoulders coiling more than the hips. It is important to realise that this coiling movement is what will give power to the shot. Many people fail to realize this and instead attempt to take the arms back without an adequate shoulder turn. The foot nearest the ball should turn slightly out as you get in position in order to stop you from shutting yourself off from the ball and the space you will need to play it.

You'll now be looking over your dominant shoulder at the oncoming ball with your racquet back and slightly higher than the ball. Your weight should be on the back foot, ready to transfer onto the front. Your swing needs to be smooth and flowing, so with loose hands let the racquet drop below the oncoming ball and swing forwards from inside to out. Aim to make contact with the ball at waist height and just in front of your body with a full, smooth outward and upward swing. Many coaches will use the expression 'stay with the ball' in order to encourage you to hit through the shot before letting your arms relax too soon on the follow-through. This will ensure that you get the power needed to achieve both depth and spin. Keep your eyes glued to the ball through the contact point and this will help you keep your head still and the shot balanced.

On finishing the stroke, make sure you bring your elbows through high so that you are looking over your non-dominant shoulder. This will assist you in making a smooth weight transmission through the ball and avoid the problems associated with a short and pushy movement. You should now be in a nicely balanced position to recover, ready for the next shot.

> **TOP TIP**
>
> 'I believe the backhand is the toughest shot in tennis for the average player. It should be one of the easiest shots but it becomes a phobia in which you think the ball is too heavy. Then you don't get your shoulder around and you don't make good contact with the ball.' Rod Laver, double Grand Slam champion (*Serve & Volley*, November 1989).

(a) Shoulders rotate with both arms extended.

(b) Eyes on the incoming ball.

(c) Racquet drops into the pre-strike position.

(d) A smooth upward swing…

(e) …causes trunk rotation.

(f) And the upper body faces naturally to the court on conclusion of the stroke.

The Single-Handed Backhand

This backhand can be considered as a mirror image of the forehand, only complicated by the need to turn the shoulders fully, in order to get your body out of the way so that the shoulder joint can swing the racquet freely.

A good starting point is the Eastern backhand grip: when you hold the racquet and run your finger down the outside left edge of the frame (right-handers) it comes into the V created between thumb and first finger. This grip allows for maximum versatility at the moment of impact with the ball. If this grip feels very unnatural for you, or if you feel that you are not able to support the racquet well enough with your wrist, try extending the thumb of your playing hand up the back of the grip. This extra support often makes all the difference in terms of stiffening up the stroke.

When taking the racquet back, use both hands and think in terms of your spare hand pulling the racquet back. This will ensure your shoulders are fully turned. Adjust your footwork by turning your hips and stepping forward into the court with your weight solidly on the front foot, and you should be in the ideal position to attack with a backhand that is either flat/lifted, sliced or topspin.

Avoid, if you can, stepping into the shot too soon. Try, rather, to take light, small adjusting steps for as long as you can, and make your final move onto the heel of your front foot. In this way, you can gauge when the moment is exactly right to shift your body weight onto the flat of this foot and be perfectly stable on the ball at the moment of impact. This will also prevent you from having to lunge off-balance into a wrongly measured ball.

(a) Eye on the ball.

(b) Knees bending in preparation.

(c) Racquet head drops.

(d) An upward strike, brushing the ball…

(e) …into a smooth follow-through.

The Flat/Lifted Backhand

For this stroke, like the equivalent forehand, the ball is struck at a comfortable height (somewhere around the level of the hips) and slightly out in front of the leading knee. The racquet is swung forwards in a whole arm action by the shoulder joint, and the general effect should be of a steadily rising racquet trajectory that swings up through the ball in a low to high lifting motion. At the conclusion of the stroke, the racquet should be around head high (or higher) and well out in front of the body before the arm is relaxed into the follow-through. Some players find it useful to keep the shoulders closed to the net throughout the stroke, as in this way they can avoid the racquet coming off the flight path of the ball prematurely.

To avoid coming off the line of the stroke too soon, practise by standing with your back against the stop netting, and play a full shadow stroke backhand without letting your racquet hit the wire at the end of the stroke. You should be able to do this by following through from the elbow in an upwards movement, and there should be no necessity to feel that you are having in any way to put the brakes on.

(a) Watching the ball and loading the rear leg.

(b) Feet firmly planted.

(c) The weight transfers onto the front foot.

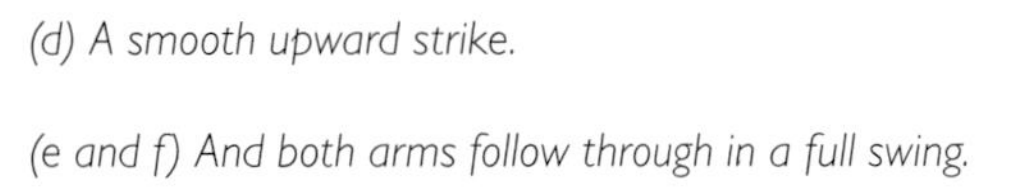

(d) A smooth upward strike.

(e and f) And both arms follow through in a full swing.

The Sliced Backhand

A natural stroke for many people, the sliced backhand is a good choice to use off a fast-paced ball, as a game changer or as a shot you can come to the net behind. With a Continental grip, the racquet is taken back higher than normal, swung forwards with a face that is open to the sky and brushed down the back and underside of the ball in a high to low trajectory. The result is a ball that carries over the net with a flat and floating trajectory while spinning back on its axis. This shot stays low on bouncing, and forces your opponent to get down to it and (hopefully) hit up to you.

The follow-through is rather in the shape of an extended concave action, which allows the ball to carry for depth. Too violent a downward stroke may result in heavy slice that is difficult to feel on the strings, and you may find yourself making too many netted errors.

(a–e) Here, the high to low racquet head path is clearly visible as the player knifes through the ball.

C

D

E

The Topspin Backhand

This stroke requires a fair amount of upper body strength for the single-handed player, but again, the real key lies not in your physique but in the racquet angle at the moment of impact.

Whether you are hitting with one or two hands, the racquet is accelerated rapidly up the back of the ball in a near vertical angle from low to high, which sends the ball fizzing over the net in a characteristic loop that hits the ground and bounces away high. Devastating when used as a passing shot or against a short length ball, this stroke in many ways epitomizes the modern game of tennis.

In order to hit it correctly, remember that your racquet has got to start from a position underneath the oncoming ball. This seems obvious, but if you're trying the shot for the first time, you might well be astonished at just how high your racquet actually is before the start of your normal backhand. Try stepping into a topspin shot and freezing just before you start the forward momentum of the racquet head. Try not to cheat. Is it low enough? If you are a long way adrift, next time you try it, see if you can imagine yourself actually trailing the racquet head on the court at the end of the backswing. You probably will still be a long way away from actually touching the court surface, but at least your racquet will be lower. Now bring the racquet brushing violently up the back of the ball, to follow through over your hitting shoulder, making sure all the while that you are perfectly balanced with your weight squarely over the front foot.

> TOP TIP
>
> 'I made it look so easy on court all those years. No one realized how hard I had to work. No one realized how much I had to put into it. They underestimated my intensity.' Pete Sampras, ex-World No. 1 and seven-times Wimbledon champion.

> KIT CHECK
>
> If you play with a lot of heavy topspin, use one of the specialist strings in order to give more bite to your shots.

As with your forehand, practise all the variations of backhand in order to round your game off with versatility and be able to cope with all conditions of bounce, pace and different opponents. Don't allow yourself to become trapped into a routine of only ever playing one type of stroke. Predictable players are easier for opponents to prepare against.

A

B

(a–f) A wide stance and good balance contribute to a comfortable low to high strike on this two-handed backhand.

The Service

The service is more than just a way of starting a point. It is a way of dictating terms to your opponent, and should be practised regularly with this in mind. After all, you don't need a practice partner, just a basket of balls and a spare court! Although the underarm service is perfectly legal, it is a low percentage shot as you can't hit it hard enough, so you should aim to build three basic serves into your armoury.

1. The flat 'cannonball' that bursts through your opponent's defence.
2. The slice that pulls them out of position.
3. The topspin that gives you a high margin for error over the net, and bounces awkwardly high.

For each of these serves, the best grip to use is the Continental. Your stance should be comfortably sideways, with your feet at approximately twenty past one position on an imaginary clock face.

The key to success on any serve is controlled relaxation. The stroke should flow through your body from your feet to the racquet head and not be muscled over the net. Simply take a comfortable semi-sideways stance to the net, hold racquet and ball comfortably together, and allow them both to fall away and then rise in unison. Release the ball into the air and relax your elbow and wrist to drop the racquet hand behind your hitting shoulder, from where it is thrown at the ball. If you have heard the old adage in the past of taking your racquet to a 'back-scratch' position, don't misinterpret this advice in the way that so many players have. The racquet scratches the back below the hitting shoulder, and not the middle portion of the lower back. Such a position prior to a throwing action would be unrealistic, and detrimental to the throwing action itself. Try it and see! You wouldn't go into that position if you actually wanted to throw your racquet out of court and over the wire, would you?

> **TOP TIP**
>
> 'You kind of live and die by the serve.' Pete Sampras, ex-World No. 1 and seven-times Wimbledon champion.

(a) Racquet and ball hand start together.

(b) As the racquet drops away...

(c) ...the ball hand rises...

(d) ...in a fluid upward path.

(e–f) The racquet extends out towards the stop netting...

(g) ...as the knees start to bend...

(h–i) ...and a classic 'trophy position' is achieved.

(j) The racquet head drops behind the hitting shoulder…

(k) …and the legs thrust upwards…

(l) …into a full body strike at the ball.

(m) Note the elevation the player has achieved.

In order to get the feeling of relaxation that you require, practise going through the movement while holding the racquet lightly between finger and thumb. This should allow you to feel how the racquet head is carried through the ball under its own momentum. Don't try and hit all the fur off the ball. In order of priority, your serve needs to achieve:

1. Consistency
2. Accuracy in placement
3. Power

Having achieved a basic service action, you can now consider the varieties of serve.

The Flat Service

In this stroke, the ball should be struck no more than 120–240cm in front of your head and at full stretch. If the grip is new to you, imagine that as you throw your racquet from behind the shoulder, your forearm should turn out (or pronate) in order to present the strings flat on to the ball. If the ball were a clock face, try and nail it right through the middle.

The Slice Service

For this stroke, place the ball a little bit more to the right and cut your racquet face around the right-hand side of the ball (right-handed players) and across your body. Again, if the ball were a clock face, try and hit it at the 3pm position. Experiment, and see how much sidespin you can place on the ball. You should try, when serving into the deuce court of an end-of-rank court, to get the ball to bounce into the side netting before it passes the service line. Remember, your intention is to pull your opponent way out of court for the return of serve.

The Topspin Service

This is best practised with an amended ball toss that positions the ball slightly lower, behind your head and over your non-hitting shoulder, as your racquet should brush up the back of the ball in order to impart forward rotation on it. If the ball were a clock face, you would be hitting across the face from approximately twenty to the hour, to ten past. An arched back may also help in this very physical shot, which should result in a high looping ball that passes high over the net, accelerates downwards, and kicks up into the air on the bounce. The effectiveness of this stroke can be easily measured by the bounce, which should cause the ball to break sharply towards the backhand side of the right-handed player.

Position of the ball place-up for:

(a) a flat service – contact will be above the hitting shoulder.

(b) a slice service – contact will be outside the hitting shoulder and at a lower point than for a flat delivery.

(c) a topspin service – contact will be above the non-hitting shoulder and at a low point to enable the upward-brushing movement.

The knee bend on the serve allows a powerful thrust up into the ball.

Where Does the Power Come From?

A powerful serve starts from the ground up and has each part of the kinetic chain joining in – from the feet, through the legs and hips and up into the trunk, through the shoulder and onwards through the elbow, wrist and fingers. Don't make the mistake of 'arming' the ball, but instead, work on your throwing action with a tennis ball by practising throwing it further and further down the length of the court. Feel how subtle changes in your positioning, the thrust upwards from a bent leg position, etc., all contribute to overall success. Watch the pros and you will notice that much of their effort is concentrated on power that stems from a deep knee bend position and drives explosively upwards, rather than forwards.

(a–g) This sequence clearly demonstrates the role of upward thrust and momentum in gaining power on the serve.

E

F

G

Some Hints on the Ball Toss

There are two schools of thought on effective placement of the ball into the air for the service.

When you are starting to develop your own style, it is probably a good idea to visualize your ball holding hand as being at the bottom of an imaginary transparent tube. You should see yourself placing the ball up the tube, without it touching the sides, and simply reaching its highest point, only to drop back down again, still without touching the sides. In order to do this successfully, you should hold the ball lightly in your fingertips with your palm uppermost. Now, with only the minimum of initial downward movement, use the whole arm to place the ball inside the imaginary tube. Keep your palm facing upwards throughout, and when your arm can go no higher, and is past the top of your head, release the ball. Note that there is no use of the wrist in the place-up and the action is very much a smooth and controlled one with no jerky movements.

The second method of ball place-up is not so easy for the beginner, and is probably best left to the more advanced player who can graft it onto his game. Here, you keep the hands together as the racquet is withdrawn into the take-back, so that the shoulders turn sharply away from the court. The ball is then released from a point approximately level with the trailing hip, in an upwards and outwards movement that places the ball out in front of the server. It can be readily seen that the effect of this is to require the upper body to violently uncoil into the service action, thus giving the stroke additional body power and punch. This additional shoulder turn can be made particular use of in the second serve, and you may find it a helpful tip towards getting more bite on your topspin delivery.

In conclusion, many people have been miss-served in the past by that familiar piece of advice to 'throw the ball higher when serving'. The net result of this has been that players can often be seen tossing the ball high into the air and then waiting seemingly an age for it to come down again. This leads to a hitch in the service motion, to say nothing of the difficulties involved in trying to hit an object that is accelerating towards you as it drops.

The correct approach is to place the ball up no higher than it needs to go in order to provide a smooth continuous throwing action with the racquet. This will probably be no more than 12–18 inches higher than the point where you make contact with your strings. Some great servers may look as if they are hitting the ball while it's rising. They're not! In reality, what they are doing is striking the ball at the precise moment when the ball has ceased rising and had not yet started its descent. Find this point for yourself by standing against the court boundary netting and stretching up with your racquet as high as you can reach (making sure the racquet is vertical in your grasp). Mentally mark the point where the top of your racquet touches the wire, and add on about 15cm to take account of your jump up into the serve. This is the height you should practise placing the ball to.

Practise the varieties of serve regularly and separately, and remember that the old adage 'you are only as good as your second serve' is very true. Unless your hard, flat service is very near perfection itself, you are inevitably going to need the extra safety margin on your second delivery that is achieved through spin and resultant height over the net. The alternative is a 'powder-puff' delivery that openly invites your opponent to smash it into oblivion.

The ball has been placed accurately in order for the player to achieve full racquet extension with the weight going forward into the court.

Return of Serve

Most people realize the importance of practising the serve, but how many times do they practise the return of serve? Yet this is every bit as important. You play just as many of these as you do the serve, so try to build this into your regular stroke practice sessions.

Obviously, your position when waiting to receive serve is very much a matter of how good your opponent's delivery actually is, but a good starting point would be approximately a racquet's length in from the sideline and behind the baseline, with your feet angled towards the server. Remember that it is always easier to run forwards and hit a balanced stroke than it is to go backwards.

Watch the pros when they are receiving serve and you will always see a split-step (little hop from a wide stance) that occurs just before the server makes contact with the ball. This is to ensure that as you land, your knees and ankles compress much like a spring that can then explode into a powerful release of energy.

Here, the player has been jammed up by a ball aimed straight at his body.

If you're facing a hard server, crouch low and take a slightly pigeon-toed stance. This places your weight in an ideal position to spring quickly to either side. Hold your racquet firmly out in front of your body with your elbows well away from your sides and when the cannonball comes through, step forwards into it and block the ball back much like a volley. You haven't got time for a big backswing, so keep your take-back to an absolute minimum on this shot.

Consider the chipped short cross-court return as a weapon, as this keeps the ball nice and low against the incoming volleyer, and forces him to recreate his own pace against you. Utilize a short, sliced punching action with minimal take-back and attempt to float the ball diagonally across court so that the incoming volleyer is confronted with a dying low bounce and a minimum of pace to work on. Similarly, if you get a short ball, either pulverize or place it depending on your confidence, but above all, don't just put it back into play! These chances don't normally come that often, so make the most out of them.

Returns down the line are a good option against volleyers, but remember that you are playing over the highest point of the net, so a dipping topspin return is a better percentage option than a slice which may sit up for the volleyer.

Use the cross-court low topspin return for safety in doubles and be alert in singles for the down-the-line approach against you. The lob may be considered now and again as a means of breaking your opponents' rhythm in doubles but, above all, the key to success in the return of serve is to know exactly what you are going to do before you try to do it!

Return of serve. Return the chip to point A, drive to point B or hit with dipping topspin against the volleyer's point C. The lob is useful for breaking the incoming volleyer's rhythm.

The Volley

The great Pancho Gonzales is reported to have said, 'A volley ain't worth a damn if you don't get it in the middle of the strings,' which is just about the best possible advice on how to improve the stroke. The only addition to this is to make sure you hit it out in front. In order to achieve these two aims, follow the points below.

The Forehand Volley

1. Make sure you are gripping the racquet firmly.
2. Work on your positioning in order to have more time on the stroke.
3. As soon as you know whether it's to be a forehand or a backhand, line your racquet up behind the oncoming ball with the minimum of take-back preparation.
4. Think of your racquet as a brick wall and let the ball simply rebound from it. Your arm should be slightly bent at the elbow in order to give the shot more solidity. There is no need for a huge swing and, indeed, this usually results in disaster. Instead, simply visualize someone standing behind you at the conclusion of the stroke. That person should be able to look through your strings and see where you struck the ball to. In this way, you will avoid relaxing your wrist too soon.
5. If you have the time, drive forwards onto the left leg for the forehand, and right leg for the backhand in order to turn the shoulders and get more weight behind the ball. (This applies to right-handed players. Simply reverse if you are left-handed.)
6. Work on meeting the ball a comfortable distance away from your body, and then use your body to achieve that same distance on every ball. Don't get into the habit of waving your racquet out towards the ball and leaving your body behind!

(a) The racquet is lined up early behind the ball…

(b) …which is watched closely through to contact.

(c) The ball is struck in front of the body with a firm wrist.

(d–f) Recovering quickly into the ready position.

The Backhand Volley

Follow the same 1–4 steps as for the forehand volley, but step forwards to meet the ball onto the right leg (for right-handers). You are more likely to make the mistake of withdrawing the racquet too far on this side, so be aware of this possible problem and work to meet the stroke comfortably in front of you, as in step 5.

Aim to position the racquet before impact with a slightly open face in order to control the shot with slice, and hit through the ball as though delivering a rabbit punch with the heel of your hand.

On both forehand and backhand volleys, get the feel of punching the stroke from the elbow with a short but explosive action, and try not to get too much shoulder movement into the action.

Finally, remember, no matter how hard the ball is struck at you, you will not get hurt provided you immediately line up your strings and play the ball as a backhand. You can always protect yourself with a backhand volley, but you will tie yourself in knots trying to hit a forehand.

(a–f) Like the forehand volley, the keys to the backhand are early preparation, a short punch attack with minimum racquet take-back, and a firm wrist.

RULES CHECK

You lose the point if you reach over the net in order to play a volley.

NIKE
NIKE
C
D
NIKE
NIKE
E
F

The Low Volley

Treat this shot in every respect like a high volley, i.e. out in front, middle of the strings, early preparation etc., but make sure that, in addition, you bend your knees and get right down to the ball while maintaining the angle between racquet and wrist. If you watch the pros play this stroke, you will notice that what they do not do is stay upright and drop the racquet; but how many times do you see this type of volley dumped into the net in your local park?

Because the ball is lower than the height of the net, you should open up your racquet face in order to impart some backspin to the ball. This will allow you to play the ball deep with control, rather than a gentle, high over-the-net return that your opponent can murder.

A good way to practise this is to balance a tennis ball on an upturned paper cup or old soft drinks can and (bending your knees) play the stroke, hitting the cup out from under the ball with the leading edge of the racquet, while sending the ball upwards and out over the net. The principle is the same as using a sand wedge in golf. (You had better do this on a grass court or outside the hard all-weather area of the court, or you will be spending a lot of money replacing your scratched and battered tennis racquet!)

If you can play a volley this low successfully, you shouldn't have too many problems dealing with the majority of low ones, but you should still work on your reaction speed in order to be able to get to the ball quicker, and before it dips. Always take the ball early on the volley when you get the chance. Below the net, shots are always going to be harder.

So in conclusion, remember to get down to the ball and open your racquet face, and you shouldn't have too many problems on this shot.

(a) Eye on the ball.

(b) Early racquet preparation.

(c) Bending the knees to get down to the low ball.

(d) The racquet face is opened…

(e–f) …enabling both net clearance and depth.

The Stop Volley

This stroke should be played from close to the net and only when your opponent is deep in the court or otherwise severely off balance. The ball should be played with an open racquet face (strings pointing towards the sky) in order to achieve the degree of backspin that will ensure the ball drops vertically into the service box with no additional forward momentum.

Where a lot of people go wrong on this stroke is in trying so hard to hit the ball gently, or even feeling they are trying to catch the ball on the strings, their wrist gives way too much and they strike the ball off-centre. Alternatively, they forget to achieve the necessary upward and back-spinning momentum on the ball and it carries too far into the court, to be easily retrieved by the opposing player.

To play the stroke, practise trying to gently pop the oncoming ball up into the air (no higher than one metre) and catching it with your spare hand. You will probably find that your early efforts fail to provide a ball you can actually catch, but instead produce creditable stop volleys!

Remember, this is a surprise shot. Don't become predictable when playing it, and always try to give your opponent the greatest possible distance to run. Therefore practise it regularly, not only in a straight, forward direction, but also on the diagonal. You will find it a useful weapon in your doubles armoury.

(a–c) At this point, the forthcoming stop volley is well disguised…

> RULES CHECK
>
> If you hit a ball with so much backspin that it bounces in your opponent's court and then returns over the net to your side unplayed, it's your point but your opponent may reach over the net to make his return, provided he doesn't touch it.

(d–f) ...until the racquet face opens and cuts under the ball with backspin.

The Drive Volley

This stroke is a difficult shot to master. Indeed, in the past many texts suggested never playing the stroke, and instead staying always with the safer and more predictable punch volley. While this advice has a lot to commend it, it's fair to say that in today's modern power game the stroke is the number one weapon of choice for many players advancing from the back court, especially so in the women's game.

Any mistakes encountered normally come from the mistiming of the oncoming ball. You find yourself approaching the net, when a seemingly floating shot drifts across the net towards you. In an effort to put real power into the stroke, the racquet is taken back as if for a groundstroke, and then swung forcibly forward. However, the normal timing of your racquet take-back is geared towards a ball travelling the full length of the court and therefore taking twice as long to reach you. In short, you rush it!

Avoid errors by practising the stroke and becoming used to the quicker take-back action. Aim to take the ball around shoulder height and avoid using it to the point where it becomes instinctive, as this will be counterproductive to your normal volleying action. This is a shot that you should only play when you have positively decided early to do so.

In producing the stroke, play off the front foot (you will probably be moving forwards at the same time) and bring your follow-through across your body, turning your wrist as you do so. You need the wrist turn to keep the ball inside the lines, as you are only driving half the length of the court. Because of this across-the-body action, your safest option is a cross-court drive into the forehand corner. Alternatively, if going inside – out on the shot – work hard to turn your shoulders early and get your feet in position.

(a) From mid-court, the preparation is like a normal forehand drive.

(b) With eyes firmly on the ball…

(c) ...a full swing is made off the front foot...

(d) ...with a full follow-through.

(e) The stroke is played as a winner...

(f) ...which we hope will not be returned.

The Half-Volley

This shot can be played from the mid-court or from further back when you are trying to take the ball early. When you're moving in on the net, there's a strong possibility that you will have to utilize the half-volley. It isn't an easy stroke by any means, so your first option should be to attempt to get in close enough in order to meet the punch volley as an attacking stroke. However, if you can control the mid-court area with the half-volley, your opponent is going to feel a great deal more pressure on his passing strokes, and you will probably pick up some cheap points on his errors.

The key to hitting the half-volley is to get down low. Bend your knees, lock your wrist and meet the ball well in front where you can see what's going on. A good tip is to visualize that your racquet face is a broom that stays in contact with the court as you push through the shot. There is no time in this stroke for a take-back of the racquet, so meet the ball firmly and push forwards on your follow-through. This stroke is well worth practising if you intend to approach the net at all, as your opponents will be desperate to keep the ball low at your feet.

Aim to hit the ball deep, and close the net down as soon as you have hit the half-volley. You don't want to have to hit again when you could have punched a winning volley away, do you?

> KEY POINT
>
> The volley is a simple shot. Do not try to make it difficult by doing more than you have to. Forget about trying to hit it hard and instead concentrate on keeping a solid wrist and a clean racquet face.

(a) Use the knees to get down to the low ball.

(b) Take the ball out in front...

(c–e) …and stroke firmly.

The Lob

The lob is a very under-rated stroke at club tennis level, and is sometimes seen as being the mark of an inferior player. Nothing could be further from the truth! Played correctly, the attacking lob is a devastating weapon that can win points outright, set up winning situations, or destroy an attacking player's rhythm. Basically, there are two varieties of the lob: the attacking or the defensive stroke.

The Attacking Lob

Play this stroke when your opponent is camped right on top of the net or is moving in fast. Treat it as a heavy topspin stroke with a relatively low trajectory that carries the ball just out of reach of your opponent's racquet and then shoots away on the bounce. Practise disguising the stroke and brushing your racquet face violently up the back of the ball with heavy topspin. Today's pros play this stroke to perfection, especially on clay, when their opponent struggles with the initial recovery phase and finds it difficult to run the lob down.

> **TOP TIP**
>
> 'Return the ball way up in the air when you're in trouble. It's the safest, smartest play in tennis.' Arthur Ashe, ex-World No. 1 (Tennis US, January 1990).

(a) Early preparation.

(b) The dropped racquet head will impart plenty of spin.

(c–f) The low to high swing causes massive ball rotation, which will give both height and penetration.

The Defensive Lob

This stroke is played for one reason only – to buy you time! You need to get rapidly back into position, so hit the ball high and deep with a certain amount of slice. There is no need to disguise the stroke, as your opponent already knows he has wounded you, so just open the racquet face to the sky and play with a high follow-through in front of your body.

Generally speaking, any lob that lands outside the service box is not bad, but obviously the deeper it lands, the better. As a general rule of thumb, if you hit this stroke from around the baseline and aim to get the ball to reach its highest point as it crosses the net, then it will fall on the opposing baseline. Practise this stroke so you are familiar with the variations of weight necessary to cope with different wind conditions, etc.

Prepare for all lobs just as if you were going to hit an ordinary forehand or backhand. allow the racquet head to get underneath the ball a little more than you would normally allow, and hit up through the shot with a firm follow-through that carries the racquet outwards and upwards.

> **KEY POINTS**
>
> When you are on the run and on the defensive and if in doubt, lob! Hit high and hit deep and buy yourself time to recover into position.

Many beginners make the mistake of trying to play this stroke from the wrist and elbow only, which does not give you the control that you need. Remember the

When pulled out of position, strike the ball high over the net.

adage that the longer you can hold the ball on the strings of your racquet, the more control you will get. In this way, you will also achieve the effective depth that you require.

Finally, whenever possible, lob both into the sun and over your opponent's backhand side. In this way you can minimize the possibility of a clean smash spoiling your (not quite) perfectly executed lob!

> **KEY POINTS**
>
> At all costs, get underneath the lob and keep it above your hitting shoulder.

Returning the Lob

When you've worked your way to the net successfully, it can be a galling experience to be lobbed and then realize too late that you cannot reach the smash you would like to make. As the ball sails over your head, you turn and run it down, only to find that although you can reach the ball relatively easily, you haven't the space to do anything other than shovel it back from in front of your body.

This is a common mistake that is easily rectified by ensuring that when you turn your back on the net to run the lob down, you chase the ball on an elliptical path. If you run directly at the ball, taking the shortest possible route, you will arrive there quickly but with no space to do anything. Better instead to start your run seemingly away from the ball, tracking it in a curved run, so that when you arrive, you come in on the side of the ball with plenty of room in which to play your forehand or backhand.

If you follow this advice, you should find that the return options open to you similarly increase. You can run past the ball, pivoting as you go, in order to drive the shot hard past the approaching net player, or you can play a perfectly balanced return lob over your opponent's backhand shoulder.

Bear in mind that having seen his lob go successfully past you, any opponent worth his salt is going to be following his shot in to the net. Therefore, you should be weighing up in your mind, as you run down the lob, whether to play safe with a lobbed return or try to take the initiative back with a surprise (though risky) drive.

If, however, you find that you are being passed with the lob often, you might consider whether, in your eagerness to get the net, you are in fact coming in too close. Try staying back a couple of metres and see if this makes any difference. If you are still being lobbed successfully from a couple of metres inside the service box, you should work on both your jump smash (as you are probably on the short side) and your reflexes, which may be letting you down.

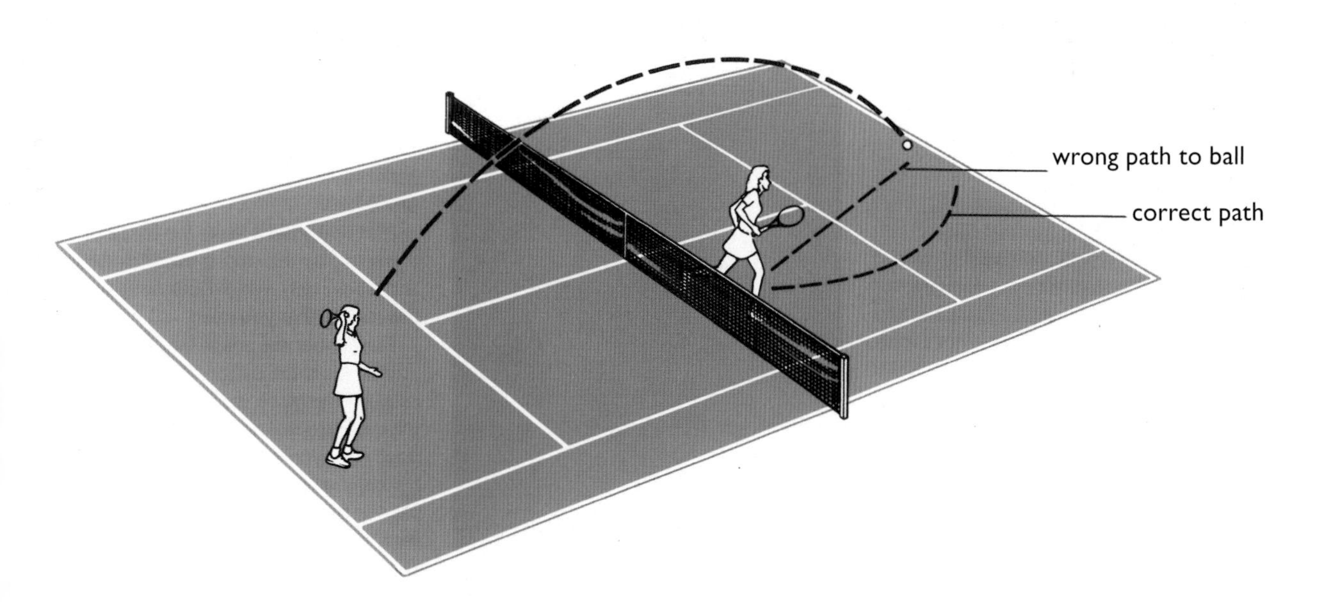

Chasing down the lob. Run in a curve when chasing down the lob and arrive with room to spare.

The Overhead Smash

The smash is closely linked to the serve, so if you have a basically sound service action this stroke should not give you too many problems.

There is one cardinal rule that will make all the difference in the world between success and failure: get underneath the ball. However, you are probably thinking that this is not always as easy as it sounds, so some consideration of how to move may help. Firstly, as soon as you see a lob going up, throw your weight heavily forward onto your left leg (right-handers), as this will allow you to spring rapidly backwards and an early start is vital in getting underneath the ball.

At the same time as you drive off this leg into a sideways stance, take your racquet straight back over your shoulder into the hitting position, making sure that you keep the elbow high. Now, work on getting quickly underneath the ball. For some people, this may mean a sideways one-foot-up-to-the-other movement, while for others it may be possible to turn the hips completely and run back while keeping the shoulders turned at 90 degrees to the net. The one thing you should not try and do is run backwards while maintaining a facing the net body position, as this imbalance may cause you to fall.

You may also find your balance assisted by raising the non-playing hand towards the sky. (Some players actually point at the ball with this hand and imagine themselves catching it in the air, as they find this acts almost like an unconscious spirit-level, letting them know that they are not yet under the ball.)

Having accomplished all this, nail it! Of course, if you're a long way back from the net, this may not always be possible, and you may well go for a placement hit with spin that allows you time to recover for the next stroke. But if you are indeed fortunate enough to be close to the net and well balanced, have a go. Treat the stroke exactly like your service and strike it out in front of your head with a full racquet arm extension and follow through across the body. Try to make your opponent regret ever considering the lob against you in the first place.

Obviously, there will be times when

(a) Side on to the net with racquet back and spare hand sighting the ball.

(b) An upward thrust of the legs.

(c) A full strike taken at maximum extension...

(d and e) ...and recovery.

When there's no time to get under the ball for a forehand smash, use your wrist to snap the shot over your backhand side.

you recognize, as you're moving backwards, that the lob is a fairly good one and you're not going to get under it easily. Under these circumstances, be prepared to jump into the shot. Preparation remains as outlined above, and you should be sure to be tracking the ball carefully all the time. The right-handed player will push hard off the right foot at an appropriate moment when this foot is nearer the baseline. As he is travelling fast towards the back of the court at this moment, there should be a definite spring into the air off this leg, the objective being to gain height on the ball. While in mid-air, the smash is played, with the left leg executing a 'hitch-kick' movement that effectively allows for both power through the ball and a smooth transition of weight into landing on this leg without any body momentum being lost.

This sounds a great deal harder than it is, and you should practise the movement to the point where you feel consistently happy to produce it without any conscious effort, otherwise you will find yourself in the same position as the caterpillar who listened to advice on how he should walk, and consequently found that he kept tripping over his own legs! Practise by standing in front of the service line, sideways onto the net with your racquet back behind your shoulder and your left arm extended towards the imaginary ball. Push upwards and backwards with your right foot and land on your left leg behind the line while simultaneously playing the smash. You'll soon get used to the feel of this shot.

A behind-the-back shot can be both entertaining and a 'get out of trouble' reaction shot.

Should the lob go over your backhand shoulder, try to run round it to take a normal smash as quickly as you can. The backhand version is one of the hardest shots in the game. However, if it's a quick, yet soft lob that gives you no time to run around it, don't despair. The minute you see it coming, turn your shoulders, bring the racquet back and bend your knees ready to jump hard into the shot. The major power element for this shot comes from the legs, so you should be ready early to really thrust upwards as you stroke. If you take the racquet back with a cocked wrist, you will be able to snap into the ball as you take it high and directly overhead. Follow through with your whole arm and, as you land, continue turning to face the net so that you're not at a disadvantage if you haven't managed to end the point.

The Behind-the-Back Shot

This seeming trick shot is really quite useful; it's played by the pros, less out of a sense of delighting the crowds (though this is definitely a consideration) than out of necessity when they have been wrong-footed.

Seen more often on the volley, the shot is played when you anticipate a return to your forehand side, and consequently turn your shoulders prematurely. Under most conditions, this early shoulder turn is to be commended, but just occasionally you will get it wrong and find that the ball has been hit to the backhand wing. With your shoulder already round, you now have little chance of getting the racquet onto the ball successfully unless you play the stroke from behind your back.

In effect, if you think of your racquet having to describe a circular movement around your body, you have the choice between making a 240-degree movement around the front to make the shot and a 120-degree movement around the back, the latter being obviously quicker.

Play the shot with the forehand face of

the racquet and maintain a firm wrist. The most important thing is to practise the movement while closely watching the racquet face. You won't normally be able to see the stroke as you hit it, so you must become totally confident in your ability to present a clean racquet face to the ball, otherwise you will be sending your shots all over the place.

Remember to practise this shot. Just because you will only have to play it once in a blue moon is no reason to find yourself at a disadvantage when that blue moon occurs. A variation on this shot, often seen when at the net defending against a full-blooded smash, is the behind-the-back and between-the-legs volley. Be careful with your practising!

The Hot Dog

To see this shot played to perfection, watch Roger Federer demonstrating it in many of his most memorable matches. Played on the run towards the back fence, the ball is played between the legs with your back towards the net. Not surprisingly, it tends to be a real crowd-pleaser.

The key elements of this shot are the Continental grip and the ability to arrive on the ball with the feet aligned in a wide stance. Practise by standing on the baseline facing the stop netting with your feet apart and a ball placed on the line. Now, just work on flicking the ball behind you. As you get the feel for this, progress to having a partner throwing gentle balls for you that you can run down and hit between your legs. Despite the fact that the shot is only rarely needed, it's worth copying Roger Federer and practising your hot dog. Winning a point with one of these shots is not only satisfying, but can also completely demoralize your opponent.

The 'hot dog' is sometimes essential off a really good lob.

The Drop Shot

There are two common mistakes to avoid when hitting the drop shot. The first of these is to try to win the point with it. Remember, the drop shot is basically a low percentage stroke. You should play it from a position inside the baseline so that your opponent has less time to see it coming, and you should view it as a stroke that is intended to allow you to win the point not outright, but on the next stroke as a result of your opponent's frantic rush to the net and resultant scrambled return. If you do actually win the point outright, see it as a bonus rather than the intended fruits of your labour!

The second common error is to try and skim the net. Remember that a ball which passes close to the net tape is going to continue travelling on for a distance before it hits the court. This is going to make it easier to play for your opponent. Therefore, aim instead to achieve a ball which crosses the net at a safe height (say 1–2 metres) and then drops vertically. This means your ball must have backspin. Your main aim is to make your opponent run the greatest distance, so you should practise by trying to hit balls that bounce no less than three times before they continue past the service line.

The way to actually produce the stroke is to treat it almost like a volley. There is no great need for either a lot of preparation or follow-through, but if you can disguise it well by making it seem that an ordinary groundstroke is coming, so much the better. Move forwards into the stroke as if you were going to volley, but take the ball after the bounce. Turn your wrist under the ball at contact and 'feel' the ball rebound off your strings. You should achieve a back-spinning ball that climbs safely over the net and then drops vertically without much forward momentum.

Experiment with this stroke as it can be a useful weapon in your armoury, but don't use it too much. Its real value lies in surprise; even the best drop shots can be reached when they become predictable!

> **KEY POINT**
>
> Spin is vital on the drop shot, so practise by standing still, dropping a ball onto the court and cutting under it so you can gently pop it up into the air with continuous spin.

> **RULES CHECK**
>
> You automatically lose the point if you inadvertently touch the net with any part of your racquet, clothing or body while trying to retrieve a drop shot.

(a) This example is being played rather too far back in the court.

(b) Preparation is as for a normal drive…

(c) ...with the racquet higher on the take-back...

(d–f) ...and the face of the racquet turned at impact to cut under the ball with topspin.

The Windshield Wiper or Propeller Drive

You know the feeling. You have just played a great forcing shot and your opponent has scrambled the ball back over the net. He's managed to get back into a covering position, but the ball is going to drop short in your forecourt and probably sit up invitingly just begging you to do something forceful and win the point. But what are you going to do? The propeller drive is a super shot for nailing the ball for a winner in these circumstances.

The normal options are:

1. Carefully place the ball very deep away from your opponent (but he may get to it).
2. Play a drop shot (but this is a low percentage shot and you may fluff it).
3. Hit the ball hard with heavy topspin (but because you are hitting to a shorter length, you may very well hit out).
4. Hit the ball with heavy slice in order to make it bite into the court on impact (but you run the risk of driving into the net).

The propeller drive does away with these problems by giving you a high percentage, attacking stroke that is perfectly suited for this position on the court. What you want is a heavily topspun shot that gives you a fair degree of net clearance and yet lands safely within the confines of the court, while bouncing aggressively away from your opponent.

Visualize your racquet as an aeroplane propeller, hitting across the face of the ball from a 4 o'clock position to 9 o'clock position, with your wrist providing the driving force. Get the feel for this stroke by starting with your racquet held out in front of you at the throat, with the face of the racquet towards the net. Now, (as a right-hander) cock your wrist sharply to the right so that the tip points to the 4 o'clock position. Without moving your arm, use your wrist to accelerate the racquet head sharply across to 9 o'clock. Now try this against a dropped bouncing ball. When you can make contact regularly and efficiently, move your hand half way down the shaft of the racquet and try again. Finally, when you have mastered this, try the stroke with a normal grip on the handle. Eventually, you should be able to hit the shot against a ball fed towards you from across the net.

Remember to really go for this shot. Its point-winning characteristics lie in the fact that it is hit hard, and therefore kicks away from the player trying to retrieve it. It's a fun shot that breaks most of the normal rules of stroke production by causing you to rely heavily on your wrist, so practise it the same way you would practise your normal forehands or serves, etc., and add a new dimension to winning rallies from the front of the court.

> **KEY POINT**
>
> Visualize making a fan shape in the air with your racquet across the back of the ball in order to hit this stroke effectively.

The propeller drive.

Hitting with Two Hands

Hitting with two hands on both wings is somewhat unusual, but there are examples of players who do this successfully. However, in most cases, exponents find the shot useful for playing on the backhand side, with the dominant hand being the one holding the racquet closer to the butt of the handle and the non-dominant hand giving enhanced stability. There are probably three good reasons for playing a stroke with two hands on the racquet.

1. You are just learning and have a very weak wrist.
2. You are a natural athlete, the stroke feels right to you and you find you can achieve far greater power this way.
3. You are a natural athlete and find you can disguise your shots easily this way.

Two hands on the racquet make backhand returns of serve easier to deal with off high-kicking balls.

Notice the emphasis on natural athleticism. This is because, played correctly, the stroke is a physically demanding one, requiring good movement skills in order to counteract the restricted reach caused by having both hands on the racquet.

If you think the stroke is for you, the keys to success are:

1. Keep both hands close together on the grip throughout the stroke.
2. Twist your upper body fully through the stroke. Using the arms alone is simply not enough as the swing is now restricted by the additional hand.
3. Work on your speed around the court.
4. Work on your ability to handle low, short balls, together with those struck directly at you, as these can be a problem. You may even find it simpler to revert to a one-handed shot on these occasions.

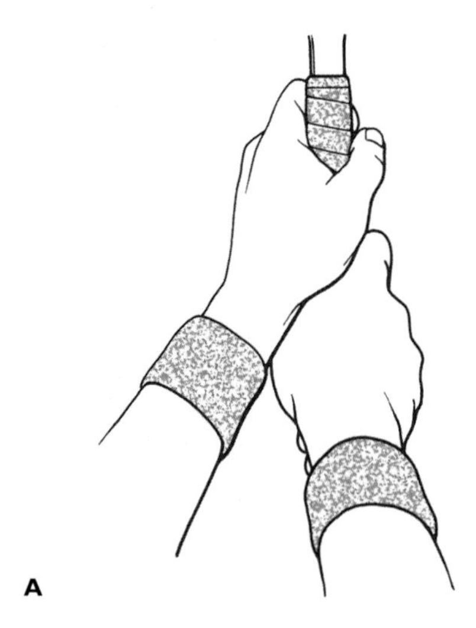

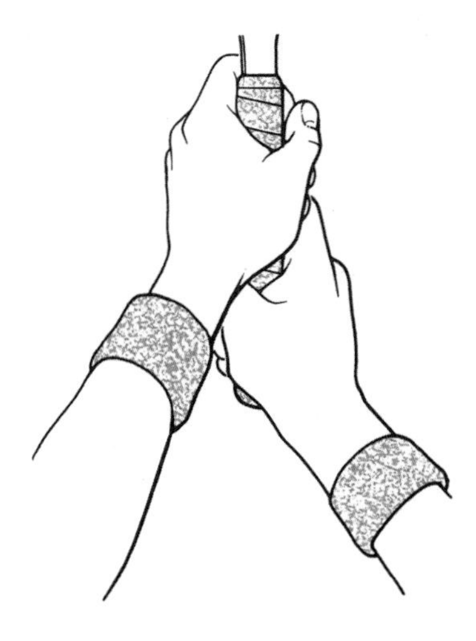

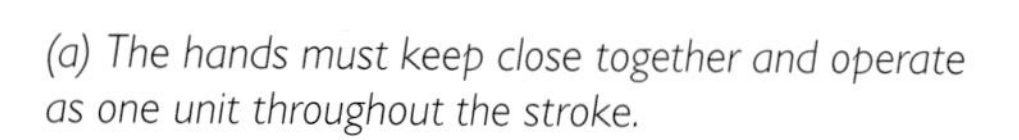
(a) The hands must keep close together and operate as one unit throughout the stroke.

(b) The two-handed backhanded grip. Here, the right-handed player's normal forehand grip is turned into a backhand grip by the simple addition of the left hand, without which this grip would not provide enough strength to hit the ball with control.

CHAPTER 7

PRACTISING

Using a Practice Wall

Practice walls in the UK have in recent years become harder and harder to find, often as a result of natural pressures on space or the fact that many of them were originally built in the 1930s and '40s and have simply become perilously unstable.

This situation is a great pity, because the regular bounce and the constant user-friendly nature of a wall make it the near-perfect practice partner. Rod Laver (Grand Slam winner in 1962 and 1969) recounts in his autobiography how he used to hit against the practice wall at home in Australia in his boyhood, both in the morning before school and in the afternoon on his return. The many solid hours of grooved stroke reproduction that this entailed were, he felt, invaluable in his development as a player.

Martina Navratilova similarly recalls many hours of diligent wall practice during her Czechoslovakian tennis upbringing, often volleying continuously until noticed by the coach, who would then invite her onto the court to join in the practice session.

There is no doubt that you can benefit from practising all your strokes (with the possible exception of the lob) against a wall. Any flat wall with a reasonable amount of space and away from windows will do, but it should be structurally sound and not likely to inconvenience anyone situated on the other side of it! A wall will return anything you hit at it, at more or less the same speed. For this reason, stand well back and let the ball bounce twice. Alternatively, use really soft balls. (You can deliberately puncture some and save them exclusively for wall work or you can purchase junior specific low compression balls.)

Use chalk marks (ideally circles) at different heights and see how many times you can continually hit the target. For creating the baseline rally feel, you need to mark a circle of 1 metre diameter about 1.8 metres above the ground, while for practising your passing shots you should aim about 1 metre above the ground. (Bear in mind that this is played as a winning shot and because of its flat trajectory will be

One of the best practice partners available – if you can find one!

much faster on its return, thus making it harder to maintain the rally). Even heavily topspun shots can be worked on in this way, but here you should really use the low compression balls in order to make it easier to maintain the rally.

Volleys are harder to practise, but a softer than normal and upwardly aimed stroke will enable you to work productively on the volley while developing your ability to concentrate totally on the ball. For a glimpse of what can be possible, seek out a YouTube video of Cara Black (ex-World No. 1 doubles player) demonstrating her reflexes by hitting an incredible 115 consecutive shots in 43 seconds.

Even the overhead smash can be practised usefully if you aim the stroke at the ground just in front of the wall, so that the ball bounces upwards in a high kicking placement (some accuracy is required here).

Used in this way a wall will provide the ideal uncomplaining practice partner to enhance your game. I wish you the best of luck in finding one!

Some Drills and Practices

The great value of drills is that, by constant repetition of strokes and strategies over a period of time, you allow 'muscle-memory' to build up in the body. Consequently, when confronted with a matchplay situation where previously you might have agonized over shot selection, muscle-memory takes over, and you instinctively play the point the way you have been practising it. In this way, you take pressure off yourself and free your tennis brain for more productive pursuits (like analyzing your opponent's weaknesses, for instance).

There is also the bonus that drills practices can be every bit as exciting and enjoyable as playing points. So take time out from your normal schedule of five minutes' stroke warm-up and then straight into a set, and experiment once in a while with 80 per cent drills followed by 20 per cent points. The benefits will soon become apparent in your match results.

Almost any number of drills exist for the specific situations you will encounter on the tennis court, and it is up to you to experiment and devise your own. Always remember, though, that to be of value drills should reflect as accurately as possible the actual situation you will experience within the game and they should reflect quality of stroke production throughout. Consequently, make sure that you carry out drills from the actual court positions where the situation would exist in a match, and help each other by indicating when a stroke is being visibly compromised. It's not much use constantly repeating a shot that is being wrongly produced, as all you will finish up with is an incorrect stroke that has been drummed into your style of play to the extent that it has become your normal style.

The following are some drills that have been proven to work and are worth experimenting with.

Drills for the Forehand and Backhand

1. Position a ball can at each end of the court, diagonally opposite each other in the forehand section, approximately two metres inside the baseline and one metre in from the sideline. Now work to place your cross-court forehand drives as close as you can get them to your target can. You will find that this close attention to a target at the other end of the court concentrates your mind very much away from your own stroke production and frees up your body to work on more important matters, like controlling the ideal height over the net or getting your footwork sorted out early.

   In this last respect, the value of aligning your shoulders with the line of your shot is demonstrated, and you will quickly come to appreciate that a shot produced with the body aligned correctly is easier to control than a shot which relies totally on the arm alone to control its direction.

   In striving to hit each other's ball can target, don't make the mistake of going for broke on every shot. Leave yourself some margin for error and play within your capabilities. It should be your intention not so much to hit the can once within every ten or twenty balls with 30 per cent landing outside the court, but rather to land 100 per cent of your ten or twenty balls close to the can but inside the court, with no direct hits on the can at all if that is the price you have to pay for consistency. As you become more consistent over time, slowly move your targets closer to the lines. Don't rush this stage, though. Remember that you want accuracy combined with consistency inside the court.

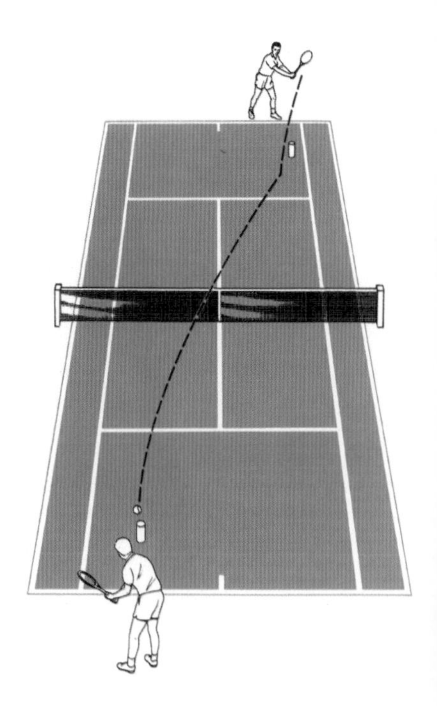

Drill using ball cans.

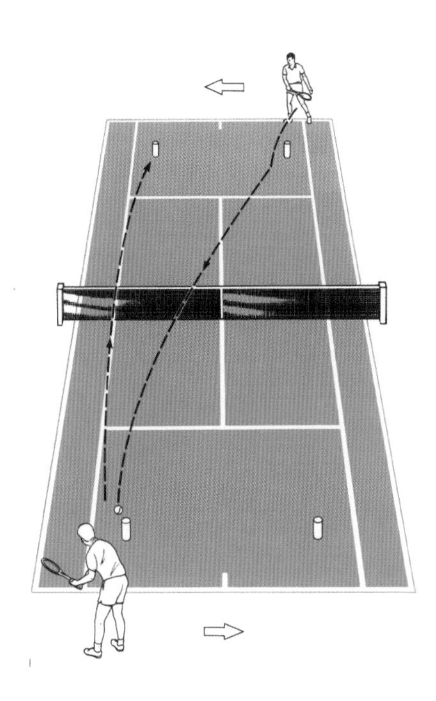

Moving across the baseline and hitting at targets. One player hits only cross court shots and the other hits only down the line

Work on systematically feeding the ball to your partner, and consider it your fault when the play breaks down on your partner's side of the net, and in this way you will both benefit fully.

Vary the above practice after ten minutes or so by moving one of the cans to a point directly opposite the other. You will now be able to practise hitting down-the-line drives on both the forehand and backhand sides. Remember that you are now hitting over the highest part of the net and down the shortest side of the triangle produced by your cross-court and down-the-line shots. Consequently, you will have to temper the length of your shots much more than you did on the previous practice in order to contain your strokes within the boundaries of the court.

Your next move should be to take the previously unmoved can and place it again diagonally opposite the first, so that you can now both practise cross-court backhand drives in exactly the same way as for cross-court forehands. Again, after ten minutes, move one of the cans to the appropriate position on the court that will enable you to practise the down-the-line shot not yet worked on.

A good, higher level variation on this drill is to mark a square of approximately 0.5 metres at each end. (Clay courts are ideal for this, as you can simply drag the mark with your foot.) Now stand your ball can targets in the middle of the square. With one person using a stopwatch, work for ten minutes trying to hit the target. Every time your partner hits the ball inside the square, he scores 1 point, but if he hits the can, he gets 5. At the end of the ten minutes, move on to the next drill as previously outlined.

By working systematically in this way, you have given yourself and your partner some forty minutes of closely directed and relevant practice that will stand your groundstrokes in marvellous stead. (If the competitive urge is too difficult to restrain, however, try wagering a round of drinks to be paid for by the player who records the least number of direct hits on the ball can – or scores the lowest level of points in the higher level drill. You may find that this focuses your attention extremely well!)

2. To continue the theme of practising groundstrokes for control, work with a partner towards keeping the rally going within the tramlines. Early preparation and footwork are vital, and you should give yourselves a realistic target which you have to achieve before moving on to something else; say twenty strokes in a row hit inside the tramlines.
3. Stand four ball cans across both ends of the court, in the positions previously explained. Now agree with your partner as to who is to play the cross-court shots and who is to play the down-the-line shots. Don't try and blast away at your target. You will easily find a rhythm that both allows you to play your stroke, and your partner to move comfortably into position in order to be able to play his. This is an excellent practice drill for hitting on the run while staying in control of your shot. However, it can be very tiring, so if the quality of the rally begins to break down, have a breather before starting again, having switched roles this time in order to hit the shot you were not practising before.

   Again, when you get better at this, play the same drill competitively, changing roles when someone achieves 7 points. Obviously, in this situation, the player with the more difficult task is the one trying to win down the line (as he has less time to recover) so it makes sense for the cross-court player to work on a slowish, consistent and accurate placement, trying to make zero mistakes. The down-the-line player, on the other hand, should be working on fast recovery footwork and a controlled, hard attack down the lines.
4. In simpler vein, give yourself an achievement target of a certain number of strokes in a row that must be hit to a depth in excess of the service line. Aim for a twenty-stroke rally before it breaks down, then forty, then eighty, and so on.
5. To make the above more competitive, set a target before which you cannot start scoring. Thus, if the target is twenty and the rally breaks down on the nineteenth stroke, there is no score and you have to start all over again. Once the twenty has been reached, though,

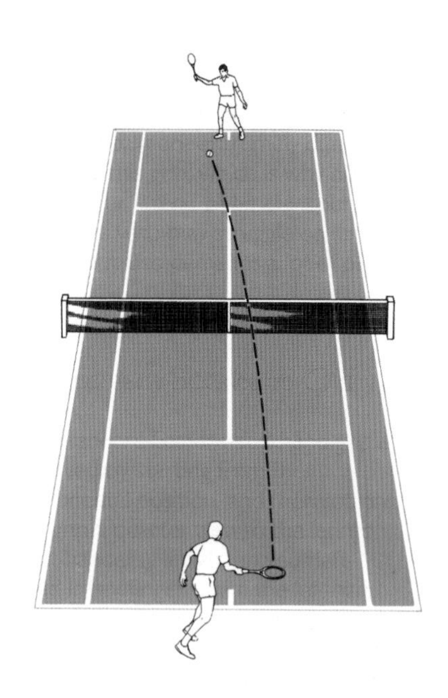

Hitting for consistency and length.

Using the alley.

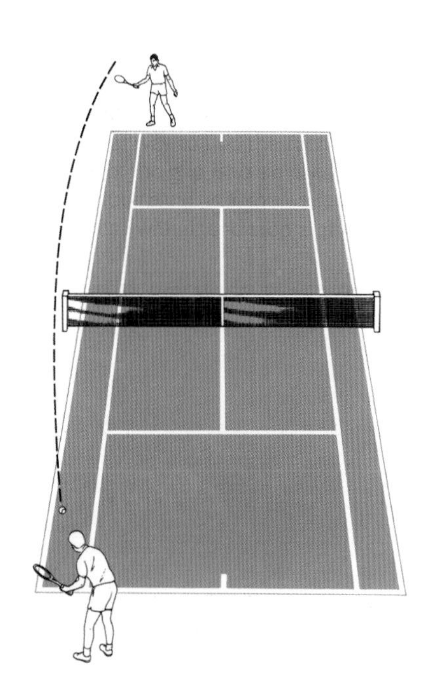

scoring is as per normal, with 15-love, 30-love, etc.

6 Similarly, decide on a figure in advance (say 100), then count the number of times the ball crosses the net in a rally. If the rally lasts for twenty strokes, then the score becomes 20-love to the person on the other side of the net from where the rally broke down. If the next rally breaks down on the same side again, and it is a fifteen-stroke rally, then the score becomes 35-love, and so on, with the winner being the first person to reach the predetermined score of 100. This is an interesting drill to work on, because you have to make decisions as you go along, such as 'Now we've got a high score, is it worth my continuing to be steady, or should I try and win the point?' or, 'I'm so far behind, is my best tactic to build up a long rally and then suddenly try and win it; or should I build up lots of small points wins, and chip away at my opponent's lead?' Either way, you learn something about your own strengths and weaknesses.

7. For dink shots, drop shots and angles, play mini tennis in the forecourt area with table tennis scoring. Service is underarm on the diagonal, and rotates every five points. No volleying is allowed, and every shot must bounce inside the service boxes. This is an excellent practice for doubles play and for footwork generally, as you have to be very light and quick on your feet. It is possible to get an awful lot of wrong-footing into this drill.

8. To work on your spin shots, have one of you hitting with topspin only, and the other hitting with slice only. This demands quick footwork in getting to the ball, but is also realistic, as you are utilizing the oncoming spin of the ball and working it to your advantage in sending it back at your opponent. It is obviously harder to return topspin off topspin or slice off slice, as to do this you have to take all the spin off the ball and cause it to rotate in the opposite direction. If

Mini tennis in the forecourt only. The whole forecourt is 'in'. No volleying allowed.

The player at the far end hits topspin only, while the player at the near end hits only slice.

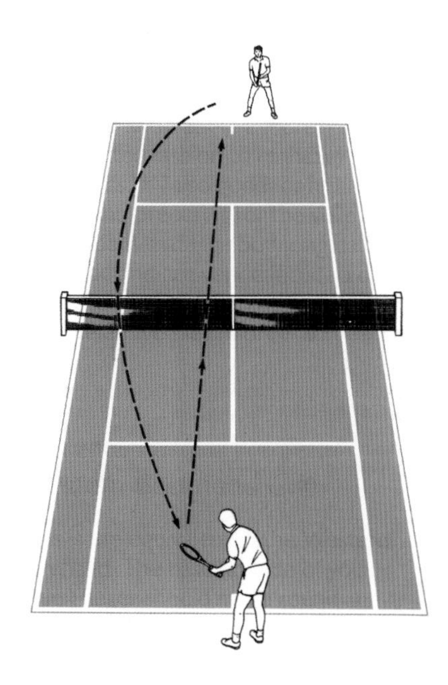

you can instead take the spin that's being given to you, absorb it, and then return it with interest, this will be an easier option.

Drills for the Volley

1. Volley rally with your partner in the forecourt area, aiming to keep the ball in the air for a minimum number of strokes – say twenty. Do this both in straight lines and on the diagonal to each other, and make sure you practise on both the forehand and backhand sides.
2. Following the same technique, pre-set a target (say 10) and, once this has been reached, either one of you can try to win the point. This can be quite exciting if you play only within a limited area (like half the width of the court) and decide in advance that the first person to 11 points overall wins the game. Another alternative that can get you over the barrier of being intimidated by the volley is to play this drill inside the tramlines only. It becomes quite a challenge to evade your opponent's attempts at winning shots directed straight at you.
3. Simply have one person practising continuous forehands or backhands from a particular point on the court aimed at the other player, who volley returns to the same position each time. Do this both in straight lines and on the diagonal.
4. One person stands at the net, and his opponent stands behind the baseline. The net player sends a very short ball over the net to simulate a drop shot, and the baseliner is not allowed to start moving until he sees the ball leave the net player's hand. On running in to pick up the short ball, the incoming player controls the ball back to his opponent, and they have a volley rally of a predetermined number of strokes. On a pre-arranged number of successive volleys (say eight), the net player lob-volleys over his opponent's head. The opponent is not allowed to play a smash and must, instead, run down the lob and return it in any way he likes to the net player, who again drop shots him, thus starting the whole sequence off again. This is an advanced drill for good players, and you should have some spare balls handy in case the drill breaks down on the volley rally stage.

   If you play this with the lobbed player trying to pass the person who is at the net, you can make it competitive by changing over positions every time the net player is beaten by the retriever's stroke. It is a very tiring exercise, as the constant forwards and backwards movement is seldom practised as much as it should be. For this reason, again, if the quality of the practice breaks down, have a breather. Quality is more important than uncontrolled (though still valuable) physical exertion.

Volley rally for control.

One at the net and one at the baseline.

Drills for the Serve

1. Some of the drills already mentioned can be started, if you wish, with a serve.
2. Combine serving practice with half-volley practice, and have one player receiving service by standing literally on the service line. This is an excellent drill for speeding up reflexes and practising the type of pick-up you often have to make from around your feet in a fast-paced doubles game.
3. Stand targets (cones or ball cans) half a metre in from the lines of the service box, and see how close you can get to them. This is a popular drill, but you should be asking yourself when doing it, 'Is my technique still sound?' It is very easy to get so hung up on the targets you are aiming for that you start pushing at your serve in an effort to direct it. Do this exercise

Serve to half-volley drill. Receiver stands on service line.

Serving at ball cans.

with a friend, and get him or her to tell you if you are compromising on your delivery. Better still, have your partner practise hitting returns of serve across court, also at a target, so you are both working constructively. Be careful about serving by yourself, for the reasons already outlined.

Combined Lob and Smash Drill

With one player at the net and one behind the baseline, the net player feeds a ball which the baseliner attempts to lob over his head. The net player is not allowed to go outside his service box in making his smash, and when one player has scored 21 points the roles are reversed. Obviously, the net player should lose every time if the lobber is playing his stroke correctly. If the smasher is consistently winning, then he is either extremely tall or it's back to basics for his partner in lobbing technique!

Drop Shot Drill

Start in close by playing drop shot to drop shot, then alternate to one player feeding and his partner drop shotting. Then, when you have both practised, go into a points situation whereby points can only be won on the drop shot, with the winner being the first player to reach 11 points.

Invent your own drills by introducing points 'loading' systems. For example, in the case of the last mentioned drill for drop shots, you could score normally, with 15-love etc., and have a double weighting for drop shots, so that every time one of you scores with a drop shot, it is worth 2 points at once. Thus, you could be love-30 down, play a successful drop shot, and move directly to 30-all. As previously stated, there is almost no limit to the number of drills and variations you can introduce to your practice sessions, so don't feel that you have to move early into playing games and sets. There is undoubtedly a place for serious points and sets play practice, but that place does not have to be at every practice session.

Warm-Up Drill

The following warm-up routine is an excellent beginning to any session, and should, in a little over ten minutes, get you familiar with the court surface and at ease with your own strokes.

Start with one player up at the net and one back.

Minute 1 – Forehand volley: Your partner hits easy controlled forehand and backhand groundstrokes to your forehand volley 'target'. Start off slowly and add a little more pace and footwork, warming up all the muscles involved when playing different kinds of volleys – high, low, right at you, a little to the side, way to the side, in front. Keep one ball in play if possible, but your partner should have one or two spare balls ready in order to keep the rally continuous. Don't try and hit hard, just work to keep the ball in play.

Minute 2 – Switch: You now hit groundstrokes and your partner hits the volleys.

Minute 3 – Backhand volley: Your partner hits groundstrokes to your backhand volley 'target'. Remember to practise all the possible footwork positions.

Minute 4 – Switch.

Minute 5 – Alternate forehand/backhand volleys: Your partner should set up alternate shots so that you can play a predictable forehand and backhand volley. Your partner should audibly say 'forehand' or 'backhand' as he sends the ball to you. Have your motionless racquet ready as a target before the ball gets there. Move your feet into position early.

Minute 6 – Switch.

Minute 7 – Overhead smash: Your partner lobs and you practise overhead smashes. Keep it easy and controlled. At first, get the feel of the ball on the racquet and stop at the point of contact. Add a slow motion follow-through after a couple of hits. Move your feet to get under the ball. Your partner should have a handful of balls and should return the overhead or feed an immediate replacement in.

Minute 8 – Switch.

Minute 9 – Forehand volley, backhand volley, overhead: Your partner should audibly say, 'forehand volley', 'backhand volley' or 'overhead' as he sends the ball to you. Try to keep one ball in play, but your partner should have some spare balls in his hand so as not to break the rhythm if a mistake occurs.

Minute 10 – Switch: After a few practice serves each, you should now be totally ready to begin to play points.

Plan your practice sessions to get the most out of them.

YONEX

PART 3

TACTICS

CHAPTER 8

POSITIONAL AND STROKE TACTICS

Using tactics correctly, and to your advantage, is the next vital step in improving as a tennis player after you have begun to master the strokes. We all develop our own individual styles of play and, together with this, our own strengths. Unfortunately, those strokes that we have worked so hard at perfecting will not be enough to continually support us when we are confronted with players of different styles, playing on different court surfaces, in different climatic conditions and with different types of tennis ball to those that we became familiar with in practice.

The starting point for tactical awareness is to fully understand your own game. Know where your strengths and weaknesses lie and how to maximise those strengths under a variety of conditions. For instance, if you are a steady baseline player familiar with playing and winning on all-weather courts, make every effort to play your matches on this surface and practise your passing shots to perfection, so that when you are confronted with a serve and volleying opponent on a grass court you can disturb him into staying away from the net, thus allowing you to capitalize on your baseline ability.

At the same time, you must develop the ability to analyse your opponent's game. Where are his strengths and weaknesses? When does he like to approach the net and does he move slowly to one side or the other? Does he wear glasses that might cause problems in very cold or damp weather? This last point should not be misconstrued as being bad sportsmanship. In matchplay conditions, you are being discourteous to your opponent if you ease up on any perceived weakness. If a player walks onto a tennis court, it is a signal that he or she is fit and ready in every way to play the game. Therefore, if a player who wears glasses finds them steaming up, or a player in worn out tennis shoes starts to slip in wet weather, this is not a signal to take things easy on them. They are simply showing their own lack of preparedness in not having demister fluid or non-slip shoes available.

Having then recognized your own game and that of your opponent, be prepared to vary your tactics according to circumstances (some of which are outlined in the following pages) and remember the basics:

1. Keep the ball in play.
2. Make your opponent run and exploit any weaknesses.
3. Show patience.
4. Continually review how your tactics are working and be prepared to change them if necessary.

> **TOP TIP**
>
> 'No matter what it looks like when you watch the pros play, it is never just blasting the ball up and down the court. A player is always thinking about how to neutralize the opponent's strengths while keeping mistakes to a bare minimum.' John McEnroe, *Tournament Tough* (Ebury Press, 1984).

Approaching the Net

Whether you approach the net only because you're forced to do so when chasing down a short ball, or because you like to go forwards whenever possible, you can influence the final result of your approach by being clear in your own mind about how you set about it. A good starting point is to think what exactly you are trying to achieve with the approach shot itself. If it's to be an outright winner, then treat it accordingly, but if it is in fact an approach shot, take more care.

This stroke should be made on the run, with your movement coinciding with a 'flow through' on the ball. Take the ball out in front of your body and steer it carefully towards your chosen target area. Remember, you are not trying to win the point at this moment; rather, you are trying to set yourself up to win on the next stroke. Therefore, aim deep, and aim either down the middle or down the same side that you make the stroke on. If you go down the middle of the court, you are forcing your opponent to create the angle on his return, and if you're lucky this may create an error. If, instead, you opt to go wide, make sure you are hitting against your opponent's weakness and then cover that side by slightly 'fading' your approach run to that side. By following the line of your own ball in this way, you will be narrowing the angle available to your opponent in the same way that an out-coming goalkeeper cuts off an attacker's chances. If, on the other hand, you try and approach with a diagonally struck ball, you had better make sure that you are an extremely fast runner, as the ground you will have to cover is that much greater. (You will, in fact, be making an approach down the longer side of an imagined triangle, which gives an opponent ages to set themselves up and pass you down the line.)

Next, time the approach so that you make your arrival 'split-step' just as your opponent is committed to hitting to one side or the other. Depending on your individual speed, this could bring you to the service line or even further in. One way or the other, you should now be in a position to volley firmly, either for an outright winner or, again, for a shot that sets you up to win on the next ball.

Provided that you follow these basic rules of approach and do not attempt any kamikaze charges forward from behind the baseline, you should achieve a reasonable degree of success at the net. If this is not the case, either change your tactics, as you are up against someone who is adept at the passing shot or lob, or turn to the section on playing the volley – you may need it!

Serve and Volley Tactics

The serve and volley tactic has to a certain extent died out in the professional game as a result of technological improvements in areas like string and racquet design, but it is still an excellent option for fast court surfaces such as grass. Here, the pace of the court makes it difficult for an opponent to chase down your shot. Also, the tactic is particularly useful on grass, as the bounce of the ball can be so unpredictable. Another important consideration is that the rallies don't last as long (this is particularly helpful for the older player who doesn't wish to be drawn into long rallies anymore).

> **KEY POINT**
>
> When approaching the net, arrive in a balanced 'split-step' position before your opponent strikes the ball. In this way you will be poised to move fast in any direction.

The starting point for effective serve and volley is to know in advance that this is what you are going to do. Too many players, trying this tactic for the first time, tend to stay back and look to see where their serve went, before running in and, not surprisingly, getting passed.

Determine which is your opponent's weak return: forehand, backhand or straight down the middle into the body. Decide where you are going to serve to, and then make your serve into the first step of your inward run. The backhand down-the-line return of serve is difficult for most players, who will normally opt for the cross-court return, so it makes sense to cover this angle slightly more on your approach.

The conventional instruction for incoming serve/volleyers is the 'three giant strides and split' technique. This suggests that as the serve is struck and the trailing leg powers through into the court, this becomes the first stride inwards, which is then followed by approximately three more, bringing the server to an area very near the service line. At this point, nearly all the published instruction advises that the first volley should be hit hard and deep so that you can then move forwards again towards the net, and pick off your opponent's weak return with a winning volley. However, observation of top players in action shows that few players adopt this advice, preferring instead to play the first volley at a very acute and short cross-court angle, thus pulling their opponent way out of position if they can get to it, but also often providing an outright winner.

Be prepared to move forward quickly when an opportunity presents itself.

Baseline Strategy

As serving and volleying has declined in the modern pro game, so baseline strategy has come to the fore. The player who wins from the baseline tends to be very strong. You can't be a consistent baseliner, playing maybe thirty or more balls per rally before winning the point, without a degree of physical fitness to fall back on. Surfaces like European clay favour staying back, as the game is slowed to such an extent that moving forwards to the net is often tantamount to tennis suicide. Also, the ball kicks up in the air, favouring the player who can hit with aggressive topspin.

The serve and volley combined can be an effective tactic.

Learning to be a consistent baseliner is an essential requirement for the developing junior player, as he or she is often not physically tall enough to approach the net without being vulnerable to the lob. Therefore, it makes sense to think through your strategy for staying back and be positive about it, rather than just reacting solely to your opponent's shots.

The incoming server needs to achieve a 'split-step' position within the dotted line in time to move to either side against his opponent's likely returns.

Serve and volley.

Probably the first point to make about staying back is that you must work on your strength and be prepared to stay in the rally for as long as it takes. Too many long rallies are lost from the baseline purely through impatience. Many players find themselves almost inevitably thinking, sooner or later, 'I should have won this by now!' and, in so thinking, hurry their stroke or try to play a winner from the wrong position.

You should recognize, in staying back, that you are unlikely to hit outright winners from this position (unless you have worked seriously on your physical strength and conditioning). Instead, you are almost jockeying for position, waiting for the right moment and the right ball to attack your opponent with your best attacking shot. This means that you should not aim your strokes too close to the lines while rallying. Certainly, you will have good days when everything seems to go right and the ball regularly skims off the lines, but it is equally certain that you will have days when those balls are consistently just a few centimetres out. A centimetre or six metres out – it makes no difference, the ball was out and you lost the point! Instead, aim your strokes to a point one to two metres inside the lines, and you'll find that your consistency in the rallies improves almost magically.

Some players prefer to dominate from the baseline.

Next, work out exactly what it is you want to achieve from the back of the court. Do you want to wear your opponent out? Or set yourself up for an approach to the net? Will you work to move your opponent around the court, throwing in drop shots and short angles in order to prevent him from achieving a rhythm? The whole point is to exert your own control on what's happening. If you deliberately bring your opponent in to the net with a drop shot, you are much more likely to play a successful passing shot than if you allow your opponent to create his own approach shot to come in on.

So, be patient, know what you are trying to achieve, aim well inside the lines, and watch the wins increase.

Creating Space on the Court

Many players are very good at rallying from the baseline, proving difficult to wear down, but they sometimes lose to players who do the same thing only better! If this applies to you, work on your ability to open up spaces on the court. The forecourt is a much neglected area for this. Lots of players are fast moving from side to side, but woefully inadequate at moving forward to the short ball. Your drop shot doesn't have to be a match winner. All it needs to do is draw your opponent forwards and force a sufficiently weak return so that you can lob into the newly created space behind him.

When you rally down the full length of the court, keep the ball returning consistently to the same area, then suddenly switch to the opposite corner. When your opponent moves across, returns, and scampers back to the middle, play the ball behind him and hopefully catch him on the wrong foot. If you combine this with a quick net approach, you may very well find a nice inviting space to hit into. In the same way, try the occasional unexpected advance on the net in the middle of a long rally. Often, your opponent will be concentrating totally on playing the ball safely to a good length, and will be expecting you to do the same. Your sudden approach on what seemed an unsafe opportunity may catch him totally by surprise; but remember, you cannot try this ploy too often.

The dominance of the topspin groundstroke in today's game makes it easier to open up the court by hitting short, angled cross-court balls off the same preparation as a deep cross-court ball. This is an excellent tactic for creating space, as it means you can take opponents out of their rhythm by forcing them to move forwards out of their comfortable side-to-side movement.

Often, a slice can be an effective way of opening up the court.

Watch the pros play this shot and see how much further it makes opponents run.

An interesting way to increase your understanding of space creation is to record a top match and later (after you have enjoyed watching it normally) re-visit the match but fast-forward it. You will see clearly the movement patterns of the players as they switch direction and force their opponent to cover increasingly greater distances as the point develops. Look for space opportunities on the court, and your game will take on new dimensions.

Percentage Tennis

The term 'percentage tennis' is reputed to have been coined by the great Jack Kramer who meant by it, simply, that you should, for 90 per cent of your time on a tennis court, go not necessarily for those strokes that you enjoy playing, but instead for those strokes that have maximum effectiveness combined with a comfortable margin of error, while allowing you to cover quickly and effectively your opponent's likely return.

For example, some players, when pulled deep and wide out of court, will go for the blistering drive down the line for an outright winner. This is fine if in fact the stroke is one of your best and you consistently win with it, but it is, for most of us, low percentage tennis.

If the shot is not an outright winner, it stands a strong chance of either being netted or landing out. Similarly, if the point is not won outright, there is a very strong chance that you have left a wide open and inviting court for your opponent to return into, simply by his taking the ball early.

The percentage tennis answer would have been to simply hit a high and deep lob that allowed plenty of time to scamper back into court and cover the open angles again. It doesn't bring the crowd jumping to its feet with its breathtaking brilliance, but neither does losing the point!

On clay, be prepared to play safe (and from behind the baseline if necessary) for as long as it takes to gain an attacking opportunity.

> **KEY POINT**
>
> Percentage tennis is about knowing your own strengths and weaknesses and relating them to the point being played as well as to the strengths and weaknesses of your opponent.

So, for percentage tennis, which ultimately means winning tennis, remember:

1. Know what your strengths and weaknesses are.
2. Don't be tempted to always attempt winning shots when out of position.
3. Don't aim too close to the lines.
4. Don't try and consistently skim the net.
5. Be prepared to break all the above rules 10 per cent of the time in order to keep your opponent guessing!

How to Gain Time

Fred Perry, in his autobiography, said something along the lines of, 'Great tennis is not about running very fast to get to the ball; it is about running very fast to where the ball is going to be!' Too many players forget this and play their carefully practised stroke, only to stand back and watch where it lands, then continue to stand and watch where their opponent hits to. This leaves you too little time to react, and before you know it you are scrambling into a defensive position.

You can avoid this situation and give yourself a lot more time on the ball by imagining an ellipse approximately 4 metres at its widest point, centred on the baseline centre-mark. Simply tell yourself that whenever you are pulled outside of this base in a defensive situation, you have to get back inside it before your shot bounces on your opponent's side of the

Play the percentages and throw up a lob if you are taken out wide.

net. In this way, you will be ready and poised to react quickly in any direction that you are pulled in. (Obviously, if you are pulled forwards from your base, you should take the initiative and continue your forwards movement into an assault on the commanding net position.) As your steadiness improves through the use of this tactic, you can start to take a more proactive approach by working harder on opening up the court.

Playing the Two-Hander

The two-handed player has a lot of advantages in achieving pace on the ball, but you can find a fair number of weaknesses in most two-fisted players that are well worth exploiting to your advantage.

For a start, double-handed players need space in which to operate. Jimmy Connors (ex-World No. 1) was the great role model for all aspiring two-handed players. His hallmark was running and running, and then running some more. Yet Arthur Ashe (also ex-World No. 1) defeated him in the 1975 Wimbledon final largely by the simple expedient of hitting the ball directly at Connors in order to cramp his blistering groundstrokes.

When the ball is hit directly at a double-fisted player, he or she has to first get their body well out of the path of the oncoming ball in order to generate any kind of pace at all, so it makes sense to do this whenever possible, and not give them the chance to knock you off the court.

Similarly, a player who hits with two hands off the volley is in real trouble when you hit a ball directly at him. The extra hand locks the racquet into position out on the backhand side, so it becomes impossible for the player to defend himself adequately. Drive the ball squarely at the body, and your opponent will be forced into a purely defensive stroke by dropping the top hand on the racquet. Thus, you will be able to capitalize on this defensive weakness and attack forcefully from the weak return.

Not quite on the subject of two-handed players, but more as a spin-off from the above point, it is quite in order for you to drive a volley hard at your opponent's body. This is the hardest area for a player to pick up the ball, and I have seen Ivan Lendl (in a match at Madison Square Garden) drive the ball directly at John McEnroe's chest and knock him over. This was accepted without comment by McEnroe, who realized that it was the safest shot for Lendl, who might otherwise have seen his passing shot intercepted.

Gaining time between shots. If you are being attacked and the shot is difficult to counter-attack from, try to get back inside the shaded area before your ball bounces back inside your opponent's court.

Another vulnerable area for the two-handed player is in the generation of pace off a slow ball. The stroke hit with two hands is usually a power stroke that feeds off the oncoming ball's pace. Deny that pace, and you should find that after a while your opponent will begin to make more and more unforced errors as he attempts to get the ball travelling at what he perceives as its normal speed.

Furthermore, the two-handed player is vulnerable when made to move forwards into a short ball directly in front of him. The same problems of lack of space occur, and a short ball particularly has to be shovelled up and scraped back across the net in little short of a defensive movement.

Therefore, watch your opponent like a lynx in the warm-up, and try to determine exactly where his two-handed weaknesses lie. You'll find it time well spent and your results will speak for themselves.

> **KEY POINT**
>
> Do not give two-handers any space in which to hit the ball. Cramp them up by playing the ball straight at them, or else make them really stretch for their stroke. Above all, do not be half-hearted about your placements.

Effective Doubles Tactics

There is more to playing doubles than simply playing your usual devastating singles game in half the court! Get to know your partner and understand the way in which he or she plays, and follow a few simple rules.

1. Understand that your primary concern is to operate as a team covering all the space and angles on the court. This overrides anything you may have been told about the importance of getting to the net at all costs. There is no point in charging to the net if your partner proceeds to stand back, as all that will happen is that a huge, inviting gap will open up between you.
2. A lot of doubles play might be described as 'diagonal singles'. The server and receiver are playing the point between them, and are both waiting for a chance to get to the net and join their partners. The net players meanwhile, are both looking for an opportunity to pounce on a poorly hit ball and volley into a space. So understand your role and look on it positively. If you simply stand back and watch in admiration as your partner rallies away, sooner or later, you are going to get 'nailed' by an interception.
3. Imagine yourself as being loosely connected to your partner by an invisible length of elastic. If he is drawn wide, move across a pace or two with him. If he falls back to cover a lob, go with him. If he charges forwards to retrieve a drop shot, go with him. Your main concern is to stop any large spaces opening up on your side of the court.
4. Recognize that the entire half of the court you are occupying is your responsibility. This means that, when starting the point, the server can stand wider than in singles, the receiver must position himself wherever he may best reach the ball, the server's partner is at the net, covering both the alley and a possible poorly hit cross-court return, and the receiver's partner is towards the middle of the court and near the service line on his side, covering both the possibility of a volley from the server's partner and a weak cross-court return from the server.

   As a general rule, if you're lobbed, run it down yourself and encourage your partner to join you in running back. If you are really sure you can't make it, call for your opponent to take it, move across to cover the side you have asked him to vacate, and let him know what to do next (usually by calling 'Stay there' or 'Switch', etc.).
5. Talk to your partner! Calls of 'Mine', 'Leave it', 'Watch', etc., aid communication and understanding between players.
6. Decide who is going to take the balls hit down the middle of the court between you. Usually, the person with the better volley will opt to take these (often the forehand player). The actual player involved is not important. What is important is that you have a planned response, as you will have to deal with this situation often in doubles. The 'divide and conquer' rule is supreme in doubles. Split your opponents up, then hit into

In doubles, talk to your partner before each point.

the gap. In order to start confusion, hit between them! When volleying, the vast majority of your shots should be aimed between your opponents. This avoids the risk of opening up unnecessary angles and leaving your partner feeling vulnerable and defensive.

Much could be said about specific tactics that you might employ, and indeed, whole books have already been written on the subject. While the above listed points provide a good generalized picture of how to approach doubles, you and your partner might like to consider trying tactical variations, such as:

1. Hold back on a hard first serve and instead employ your second serve to get to the net (it gives you more time).
2. Chip the service return short and wide to pull the receiver out of position.
3. Lob the net player on return of serve.
4. As server's partner, 'poach' (move quickly to intercept) early on in a match to worry your opponents.
5. As receiver, drive hard at the net player early on in order to test their volleying ability.
6. Play on the weaker opponent.
7. Hit your service return low and wide rather than down the middle.
8. Volley to your opponent's feet.
9. When all up at the net, try the lob volley.
10. Play your smash between your opponents.
11. Bounce your smash over your opponent's heads if they are covering well.
12. Employ the stop volley for variety.

Finally, enjoy your doubles. Remember, you're going to be playing it a lot longer in your life than singles. The age of top doubles players is significantly greater than that of singles players, and as a doubles player, like good wine, you improve with age!

In doubles the 'I' formation means that the receiver will have to guess which way the net player is going to break.

TOP TIP

'Communicate with your partner. It will keep you looser, more relaxed and it lets your opponents know that you are working together as a team.' Martina Navratilova, ex-World No. 1 and multiple Grand Slam winner (*Tennis My Way*, Penguin, 1983).

KEY POINT

In doubles, the maxim is divide and rule. Work as a team with your partner to minimize the exposure of space and weakness on your side of the net.

CHAPTER 9

PROBLEMS

Controlling Nerves

Everybody on a tennis court has nerves at some time. The trick is to control them. Being in a winning position with a couple of match points in your favour is no time to discover that nerves change your style of play. Therefore, after a series of matches take the time afterwards to write down exactly where it was that you felt nervous. Also, try to remember what you did as a result. Did you start pushing the ball? Did you start over-hitting? Armed with this information, you can now start to do something positive to minimize the effects of nerves.

Take time between points to clear your mind.

> **TOP TIP**
>
> 'When it comes to choking, the bottom line is that everyone does it. The question isn't whether you choke or not, but how – when you do choke, you are going to handle it.' John McEnroe, ex-World No. 1 (*Tournament Tough*, Ebury Press, 1984).

Next time the rush hits you, try the following:

1. Slow down and take your time over everything.
2. Take deep breaths before each point.
3. Take your mind off the score by focusing purely on the ball. Try and read the brand name on the ball as it comes towards you. Alternatively, try saying 'bounce' underneath your breath at the precise moment the ball hits the court, followed by 'hit' at the precise moment you make contact.
4. Aim to hit your shots as placements with depth and pace. (This means not going for outright winners irrespective of your position, but instead, aiming a minimum of 1 metre from the lines.)
5. Remember, the only opponent you are playing at these times is a ball. It will do exactly what you want it to do if you get yourself in position early and let your body play the stroke and not your nerves.

Don't confuse nerves with attention to detail. Rafael Nadal is notorious for his insistence on rituals like ensuring that all his drinks bottles are lined up with the labels facing the end he is playing from. Similarly, he always touches his nose and ears in a particular sequence before serving. Does this mean that he is nervous, or worried that if he doesn't get it right, he will lose the point? It doesn't seem so, as he appears to recognize the humour in the situation when opponents draw attention to the rituals.

However, you should certainly not seek to copy this behaviour. Who needs all those extra things to worry about when playing tennis?

Playing in Front of Crowds

This is one very specific area where nerves can creep in. Surprisingly it can sometimes happen unexpectedly, as in when you are playing a tournament alongside a show court with a large number of people watching another match. Maybe one player needs a toilet break and suddenly all those people have nothing to look at other than your court! The sudden realization that all those eyes are now focused on your forthcoming second serve can be a pretty intimidating moment.

The best thing to do under these circumstances is to laugh about it to yourself. You can't do anything about it other than play your game in the full and certain knowledge that, as you get better and your game improves, you will experience crowds more and more and get more relaxed about dealing with them. After all, if they're choosing to watch you play, you must be doing something right, mustn't you?

Make Match Point Count

Match points are moments of intense

Use end changes to focus your thoughts on the positive and never the negative.

pressure, when all your carefully worked out strategies can inexplicably go out the window. Similarly, game points, tie-breaker points and set points can hold the same stresses.

The secret to correcting this apparent breakdown in your game lies in knowing specifically why such breakdowns occur. Consider which, if any, of the following is letting you down at vital moments:

1. Strokes: there is a strong possibility that one or more of your strokes is breaking down under sustained physical and mental pressure. Which is it? With many players, the second serve lacks depth, pace and penetration at this crucial moment. Try to keep a record of what strokes let you down at pressure points and then you will have something concrete to work on.
2. Strategy: if you are in command, don't change your game! Also, try to play high percentage but attacking tennis. This means keeping the ball deep while not trying to achieve too much too soon. Many people freeze at these moments and start pushing the ball back, thus allowing their opponent (who after all, has nothing to lose at this stage) to start attacking with confidence.
3. The Afterpoint: many players experience problems immediately after a crucial point. If you have given your all on a pressure point, both physically and mentally, it can be difficult to match those peaks of attention in the immediate aftermath. Therefore, be aware of this and try not to become too emotionally bound up in what is, after all, something in the past that you no longer have any control over.
4. Physical Changes: be aware of your body. Do you walk faster, breathe more quickly, relax your posture and let your racquet/shoulders droop? As already stated, keep your game on an even keel by not allowing sudden change to be introduced at this vital moment.
5. Mental Attitude: be positive and avoid thoughts like 'I'm so bad!' Keep your attention on the here and now, and don't dwell on either the possibility of defeat or how exactly you managed to lose all those other points. Similarly, don't think, 'Well, mustn't double-fault now,' as this is a sure-fire guaranteed method of ensuring that you do indeed double-fault. Instead, visualize an accurate medium-fast, well-placed delivery, and you will stand more chance of success.

In summary, learn to know your game: its strengths and its weaknesses. If you have a clear idea of exactly which area it is that breaks down at crucial moments, you can learn to play the big points with confidence and avoid the self-doubt that goes with unexpected changes in the natural rhythm of your game.

What to Do When You Are Losing

When you're losing badly, change your strategy. A surprising number of players fail to follow this elementary advice. You have nothing to lose, as it looks as if the match itself has already gone down the pan. Think basics: if you've been coming to the net a lot, stay back; if you've been trying to play steady, break it up with drop shots and angles; if your opponent creams your best shots, give him nil pace to work on – but above all, change.

You could of course do nothing, and hope that either your opponent's hot streak burns out or he gets nervous and starts making more errors than you, but this is essentially negative thinking and leaves you at the mercy of external forces. Better by far to attempt to influence those same forces and, if it doesn't work, acknowledge that on that particular day your opponent was the better player.

Remember, each match is a learning experience!

Covering up a Weakness

Regrettably, most of us are not equally strong on all our strokes, and our opponents will be looking for these weaknesses during the warm-up and the early stages of a match. Obviously, a weakness on the volley is dealt with by staying back, and equally obviously, major stroke deficiencies should be worked on by taking lessons and getting the stroke up to scratch, but we should still have a strategy for minimizing the risks caused by an obvious stroke weakness.

For many players, the backhand is not as natural a stroke as the forehand, and this feeling of discomfort manifests itself by pushed rather than stroked returns. Consequently, attack off this wing becomes difficult. In order to overcome this problem and give your forehand more of a chance to win points, follow these simple guidelines.

Firstly, if you can keep your opponent pinned on his baseline with deep, high-bouncing balls, he will find it relatively difficult to attack your backhand and will feel constrained to float the ball back to you, similarly high and deep. This gives you a chance to move around the backhand and play the more forceful forehand stroke.

Next, when you're receiving service, stand a little way over to your backhand side. This cuts down the angle open to the server against you, but does leave you slightly vulnerable on the forehand against a big server.

Finally, when you yourself are serving, stand well across when you serve to the backhand court. If you stand approximately half-way between the centre mark and the tramline, you make it much easier to serve against your opponent's backhand. For most players, the backhand down-the-line return against a hard service is an extremely difficult ball to keep in court, and anyway, they will be tempted to play safe and return into the seemingly inviting space you have left exposed. Little do they know that this is just the return you want, in order to play your cross-court forehand drive! (However, you had better make sure that your speed off the mark is good enough to reach the occasional down-the-liner that gets through your defences.)

When serving to the deuce court, stand up tight against the centre mark and serve down the middle of the court to the backhand. You should in most cases be able to swiftly step around the return to your backhand and send a forehand cross-court into the backhand corner. Today's pros are masters of the inside-out forehand, and it is remarkable to see the extent to which they move across court onto their backhand sides in order to be able to play this aggressive attacking stroke.

Coping with Cheats

The outright cheat is relatively rare in tennis. Rather, the opponent you are more likely to meet is the one who so desperately wants to win the point that he wills the ball to be out. Thus, anything landing remotely near the lines genuinely appears to him to be out and in his favour. If you have the misfortune to meet the genuine dyed-in-the-wool line cheat, however, you will recognize him or her by several distinct clues.

1. The call is always at a relatively crucial moment, possibly at 30-30 on your service, for example.
2. The actual landing of the ball is often screened by your opponent's body.
3 The genuine feeling of surprise the call elicits in you (most players have an instinctive feel for the good ball).

If you find yourself at the wrong end of this situation, do not allow it to get to you, for this is precisely what your opponent wants. Instead, let it happen a minimum of twice so that you are absolutely sure, then ask your opponent if he is sure. If he answers yes, ask to see the mark on a clay court. If no mark is available, then ask the referee to come to the court. If you have to call the referee, he or she will almost certainly rule in your opponent's favour, because the convention is that players are responsible for calls made on their own side of the net. However, you will now have an official keeping watch for you and this should discourage any further deliberate cheating. If the referee cannot stay court-side, then you should ask for the match to continue under the control of an umpire. Failing all this, I'm afraid you have little choice other than continuing to play your own game or defaulting the match (which ultimately rewards the original cheating behaviour).

While the cheat is someone who consciously breaks the rules, the gamesman is more likely to try to use all the rules to his advantage in order to try and break your concentration. Therefore, simply be aware of this, and present an unconcerned face. If he wants to talk to you and discuss the linesman's decision after every point, walk away. If he points out to you that your shirt is against the rules because of the size of its logo, smile and change it. One way or another, you're not going to let anyone spoil your principal reason for being on the court – to simply play to the best of your ability.

Playing in the Heat

The Australian Open has the reputation for being the Grand Slam event most often played in unbearably hot conditions. Play has been recorded at temperatures of over 140 degrees Fahrenheit in the sun and 109 degrees in the shade. Not surprisingly, problems were experienced with this.

The first obvious thing to say is, if you

are confronted with temperatures like this, don't play. Find a pleasant shady bar or something, but forget tennis; it is simply too dangerous to take chances in such heat.

On days that are still hot, but not excessively so, take sensible precautions:

1. Carry a 2-litre bottle of plain water onto court with you, and sip from it continuously.
2. Wear a hat.
3. Carry a change of shirt if possible.
4. Ensure your racquets are gripped well, and carry replacement tape.
5. Use sun-screen for your lips and lotion for the face, back of the neck, etc.
6. Consider using electrolyte replacement drinks and magnesium if you suffer from cramps.
7. Use your full time at end changeovers.

Stay hydrated.

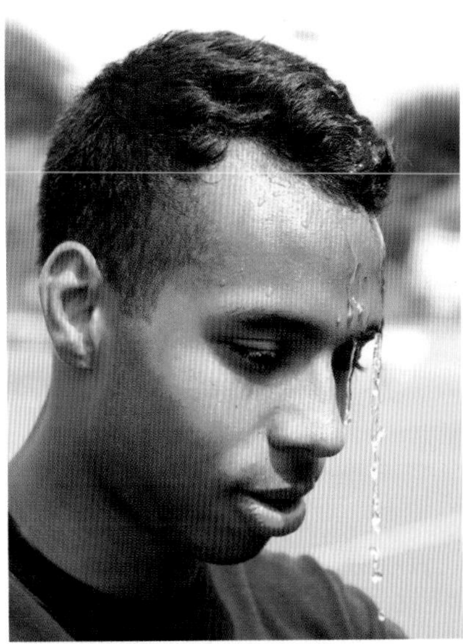

Do what it takes to stay cool.

> **KIT CHECK**
>
> Pack spare wrap-over grips in your bag to use when the heat makes your old one feel slippery.

Playing in the Cold

Playing in the cold presents few problems if you are prepared. Balls will tend to stay low and feel dead on the strings, so be prepared to bend the knees more and work hard at centring each ball onto your racquet. Looser strings may also help, as high tensions tend to contract more under extremes of cold.

Prepare carefully with routine stretching exercises beforehand, and wear modern sports clothing that provides good heat insulation combined with the ability to wick moisture away from the body. If using older-style cotton-based clothing, wear a loose tracksuit over several thin layers that you can peel off progressively as you warm up. Hands may become painful as skin splits and opens up, so prepare for this with barrier cream

Keep a towel nearby to dry your grip and racquet hand.

beforehand and a roll of surgical tape (plus scissors) in your kitbag.

Light runners' gloves will still grip your racquet if it is wrapped with one of the proprietary rolls of grip-tape available, but you should discard the gloves as soon as possible so that you maintain maximum feel on the racquet. Carry some lip-salve to guard against wind chill, and also a hat.

In this way, tennis can be enjoyed in all but the most extreme conditions, and as a result your game will improve that much more quickly.

Take care on slippery courts.

Playing in the Rain

Playing in the rain in the UK is an unfortunate fact of tennis life, and while it is not something that concerns the major tournament players, it is a regular occurrence at club and parks level. There is really very little you can do to alleviate the situation other than by wearing a hat if you are a spectacle user or, better still, contact lenses. The only really valuable advice is to shower and get into dry clothes immediately after the match in order to minimize the risk to your health. Always dry your strings after playing in the rain. Other than that, try wherever possible not to play in the rain!

Playing in the Wind

Playing in the wind is one of the most discouraging experiences for any tennis player. Carefully worked-on strokes disintegrate, placements evaporate and tempers become inflamed. So, if you have a choice, consider not playing until conditions improve. If however, you simply have to play, there are some basic considerations that may improve your chances of winning.

> **KIT CHECK**
>
> When playing in wet conditions, have a spare pair of shoes with a good grip ready and, if you wear spectacles, have a hat with a brim and some demisting agent in your bag.

1. Remember that the flat hitter is at a disadvantage. Balls hit flatly will be affected by cross winds, will sit up and float on a following wind, and fall short in a head wind. You need some form of spin to bite into the wind and keep the ball in court.
2. With the wind coming from behind you, there is the possibility of a sliced ball, carrying long, so topspin is a sound choice as it cuts down into the court. However, the well executed slice will carry deep, stay low and shoot through, so base your decision on your own strengths as regards stroke production.
3. When hitting into the wind, you are better advised to hit with slice in order to keep the ball low, as all but the most powerfully struck topspin shots will sit up short and almost beg to be pulverized by your opponent. The exception, however, is when hitting against the advancing net player, for here you need to keep the ball dipping at his feet, and a slice may well be just the right height for a volley.
4. In a cross wind, use the wind as an aid. If your opponent is out of position on the side the wind is coming from, hit across court and make him work harder to chase the ball accelerating away from him. Likewise, aim your down-the-line passing shots deliberately wide to allow them to curve back into court behind your opponent.
5. Use the drop shot a lot, and only into the wind.
6. Be careful if you lob into the wind.and use topspin on the stroke when the wind is from behind.
7. When serving, adjust your ball toss and hit with spin. Save the flat cannonballs for when there's a good following wind.
8. Give yourself time by being ready for the unexpected. Prepare early with a shortened take-back for ground strokes and stay light on your feet to the very last moment.
9. Finally, remember that the wind may be artificially cooling your body. Use sunscreen on a bright day or you may well get badly sunburned. Still want to play in the wind? Good luck, you're going to need it!

Playing Indoors

The first thing to remember when playing indoors is the fact that the light is intrinsically different. You will quite simply not see the ball as well as you normally would. For this reason, your preparation must be earlier than usual, and impeccable in its quality.

Secondly, you will possibly be unconsciously restrained on your ball toss during the serve. The sight of a ceiling rather than the wide open outdoors when you place the ball up for the service action will often result in the early stages in your holding back on the throwing action, often without actually realising it.

Drop shots often do not work as well indoors, as increased traction allows players to scurry forwards faster, and the elimination of fears about injury also contributes to a more committed approach. For this reason, you should make your short balls acutely angled in order to capitalize on the lack of space normally found between adjoining courts. Running your opponent into the side netting is not bad sportsmanship. Under the circumstances it is wise tactical play.

Smashes are easy to miss-hit indoors for the same reason as service errors. You should carefully warm up your serve before beginning to play for real, and pay particular attention to the ball, trying not to let it drop too low before you strike it. This is a classic indoors error, and if you are not careful you will find yourself hitting a surprising number of overheads into the net.

You should also pay attention to the alignment of the lights on your court. Many indoor courts have a lighting arrangement that sees the lights offset slightly to the sides of the court. If you lob down the line, therefore, you will often be placing your ball directly into the glare of the light as far as your opponent is concerned. Capitalize on this and lob down the line 90 per cent of the time when your opponent comes to the net. By the same token, it is not uncommon to find courts with large air-conditioning units positioned overhead in exactly the path of your best lob, so check out the court you are playing on thoroughly during the warm-up.

In this way, you can overcome the difficulties of moving indoors and make your tennis more rounded and varied at the same time.

PART 4

FITNESS

CHAPTER 10

THE MENTAL STATE

Tennis is a game of stress, both physical and mental. Leaving aside the obvious demands made on the body in terms of tiredness, increased need for oxygen, explosive muscle strength, etc., there are also the sudden emotional highs and lows caused by winning or losing individual points, by surviving a match point, by double-faulting or by a disagreement over a line call. Such incidents may lead unconsciously to acceleration and strengthening of the heartbeat, a rise in blood pressure, a release of glucose from the liver, the secretion into the blood of a small amount of adrenalin and a relaxation of the muscles in the bronchial tubes to allow for easier breathing.

Obviously, these physical changes taking place in the body will directly influence the body's ability to perform the strokes in exactly the correct way in which they were originally practised (which was more than likely in a stress-free situation on the practice court with a helpful coach in attendance).

At the same time, the higher centres of the nervous system are involved and it becomes true that continued repetition of practised strokes actually requires less concentration and frees up the body into more reflexive and economic movement.

Psychologists say that there are two hemispheres in the brain, one of which is thought to control what we do in a logical and analytical function, while the other processes information in a more spontaneous and immediate fashion. What this means for the tennis player is that while conscious, analytical, concise practice will get you a long way in developing your strokes, it will possibly cripple you in a match situation, when you should be performing much more on the instinctive level. That awful paralysis by analysis is familiar to a lot of match players who find themselves thinking almost out loud to themselves: 'Now, if I just place the ball a shade more to my left and arch my back a little more while I bend my knees…' and then they are surprised to find they have served a double-fault!

Obviously, every individual is different and every individual's reaction to different stresses determined by different situations in tennis is going to be equally different, so what can be done about it? For a start, we can strive to attain a positive mental attitude. This relates to our control over the levels of motivation, pressure management, concentration, visualization and self-confidence.

Have everything you need to stay mentally and physically focused on court with you.

Motivation

Knowing exactly where you want to go is half the problem, because it determines how hard you are going to push yourself, and this is where the setting of short-, medium- and long-term goals comes in. It

> **TOP TIP**
>
> 'Hey, nobody beats Vitas Gerulaitis seventeen times in a row!'
> Vitas Gerulaitis at a press conference in 1980, on being asked how he went about beating Jimmy Connors after losing to him in each of their previous sixteen matches (Tennis (US), January 1990).

is obviously not realistic to make your only goal in tennis to win Wimbledon, because for a very long time you will have no means of measuring it, other than by the fact that you have so far failed. If, on the other hand, you make your immediate goal to beat a particular friend, you have something achievable within reach from which, once achieved, you can set another higher target – for example, to play for the club.

As each small objective is reached, the continual build-up of confidence makes the next objective that much easier to gain, and so you logically press onwards to the ultimate achievement of the originally set long-term goal, which was to win Wimbledon. Start by writing your goals down but, most importantly, achieve your short-term goals, the ones that you know you can achieve with a little hard work and effort. Do not be either too hard or too easy on yourself.

The simple act of knocking the clay out of your shoes is a practical way of staying focused on the point to come and not dwelling on what has gone before.

Pressure Management

Pressure management is more than just learning to relax when you feel the pressure of big points.

First, you should identify the ideal point when you, as an individual, play well, being both charged up yet still under control of your emotions, your body and your game. It is perfectly possible to be so slow in rising to pressure that you do not respond with the immediacy demanded in order to raise your game. Admittedly this is a rare situation but it was frequently noticeable that when John McEnroe got angry (seemingly with himself, the court, the officials and the world in general) he would frequently immediately serve an ace.

If you find yourself in this situation – just unable to get going, not timing the ball correctly, being unable to concentrate, etc. – try to bring yourself back into the game by increasing your breathing rate, taking short, quick breaths. Clench and unclench your arm and leg muscles successively, take jogging steps on the spot, but primarily get your body moving.

If yours is the reverse problem and you find yourself choking on the big points, you will have to learn to relax. Slow your breathing down and take long, deep breaths. Try to co-ordinate the moment you strike each ball with the moment you exhale. Try to play the ball rather than your opponent and do not hurry your strokes at all. Above all, concentrate.

Concentration

Concentration seems like such an easy thing to do, but unfortunately it is far from easy. How many times have you heard people telling themselves to watch the ball? Surely nothing could be easier? But how hard were they watching the ball? Did they see the seams on the ball as it came towards them? Could they read the brand name on the ball as it crossed the net towards them?

The degree at which we concentrate is totally flexible and can be worked at. Obviously, you should clear your mind of anything not immediately concerned with your game. Off-court worries and problems are bound to get in the way of good tennis. Focus your attention on the present rather than the past or the future and play only the point immediately confronting you. So often, a player who is doing well visibly crumbles after a poor point and drops several more in succession, solely through thinking about that one bad point, rather than forgetting it and getting on with the task in hand.

If you watch the pros, you will often notice the little rituals they go through at the conclusion of a point. These have often been taught to them and may involve paying close attention to their

Many players gather their attention in a last moment of concentration while bouncing the ball before serving.

strings and straightening any misplaced ones, or simply turning away and using a towel. Maria Sharapova has a very involved ritual, involving forwards and backwards steps. The point is, they are all used to free up the mind from whatever has just happened, in order to focus on the next point.

Good concentration habits are born on the practice court and it is here that you should work hard at focusing strongly on every ball you hit. Practices that force you to aim at a target or cross the net a certain number of times are invaluable, as are quick movement reflex drills such as maintaining a volley rally for a certain number of strokes. If you can improve your concentration, the benefits to your game will be quickly noticeable.

One technique used by some players successfully is meditation. In simplistic terms, our essential self can be compared to the bottom of a lake. When waves lash the surface of the lake, the bottom becomes invisible to us as the water becomes muddied. In the same way, our essential self is usually obscured from us by the everyday workings and agitations of our minds. The purpose of meditation, therefore, is to produce a calming influence on that lake.

RULES CHECK

Play shall be continuous from the first service until the match is concluded, but you are allowed a maximum of ninety seconds for a change of ends, or two minutes at the end of a set. Use this time to apply your concentration.

Meditation is profoundly simple. Zen Buddhist technique employs such methods as simply paying attention to breathing, or to the sensations of walking. The principle is that this constant looking 'inwards' acts to eliminate the 'muddying' effect of our over-active, conscious minds. The result is a feeling of harmony between body and surroundings, which in turn leads to a feeling of invincibility on court. Meditation can be practised in busy or quiet areas (such as locker rooms), and is worth investigating if you are looking for that extra edge that the correct mental state can bring to your game.

Use the changeovers to focus your mind.

Visualization

Successful salesmen and successful athletes (it was discovered in a study at the University of California in 1987) have one thing very much in common: they visualize their task in advance fully and completely in their heads. The top salesman, before going in to see a prospect, runs through in his head the whole meeting, from the initial handshake, the clothes he will be wearing and the words of greeting he utters, right through to the order received in his briefcase and the office door closing behind him on his way out. Sprinters similarly see and feel themselves on the block, experiencing the moment of stillness before the gun goes off, right through to the feel of the tape on their chest as they cross the line.

This ability to think in pictures does not come easily to everyone, but it can be practised. Try to get a video film of yourself playing so that you can improve the accuracy of the mental picture you have of yourself performing. Look at videos of the pros playing and compare them with your own. In learning a physical skill, it is often true that a picture is worth a thousand words. Take some time to discover when you can most easily visualize: in a quiet room or in the open? Can you mentally see things in colour? Can you experience smell and hearing? Like time spent on the practice court, the more you practise, the better you get at it. Learning to see yourself mentally performing in the ideal way will enable you to feel you have more time available on court between strokes and will ultimately be beneficial in contributing to the building up and enhancement of your self-confidence.

Self-Confidence

Feeling good about your game, about your reasons for being on the court, about the enjoyment you are experiencing – these are all part and parcel of self-confidence. Not a great deal separates the top ten players in the world from those ranked around fifty, but the real difference is in how those top ten players feel about themselves. When they step out onto a court they know they are going to win. This is in turn seen by the opponent, who instinctively knows that the other player is thinking this and performs perfectly to expectations. (Obviously this is a gross simplification of the situation, but in essence it remains true.)

So how do you become self-confident? Firstly, do not set yourself difficult targets like the one quoted above. Instead, tell yourself, 'I can play well, and I will!' This is enough of a short-term goal to be realizable. Next, improve your physical training. The stronger and fitter you are on the court, the better you will feel about yourself. Set realistic, achievable goals and constantly update them. Remember that success must be measured purely in terms of the contest with yourself. Here, you can always win and thereby gain the foundation to build upwards towards even higher and higher goals.

With self-confidence and a positive self-belief, even trick shots will become easier to attack.

CHAPTER 11

THE PHYSICAL STATE

You can lose a match because your opponent was better than you on the day. You can even lose because you employed the wrong tactics, but the one thing you should never do is lose because you were not fit enough. If you know that you can stay out there as long as it takes to win a match, that is simply one less variable to worry about, and you can concentrate on something much more important – like winning.

Physiological Requirements of Tennis

Tall players have won Wimbledon and so have small players. There have been thin champions and even the occasional, if not fat, then certainly rounded individuals (more often in doubles). The fact is that physically there is very little stopping most people performing the game to a high level. If we look at the current top competitors there are similarities (the players tend to be taller with broad shoulders and well-defined thigh muscles), but there is very little to differentiate the top tennis player physically from any other individual in the peak of health. So what specific demands on our bodies does the game make? It asks for suppleness, strength, stamina and speed, combining agility and muscle endurance.

Suppleness

Suppleness or flexibility is vital to the tennis player who needs the ability to move the various parts of his body through a full range of movements often at full stretch. Injury is more likely when a joint has become stiff either with age or disuse. Often people realize this almost unconsciously, and immediately on walking onto the court commence a vigorous bouncing/stretching routine. To be of benefit, it is important to do this correctly.

Whereas it used to be recommended that slow stretches were the best way to warm up, it is now felt that stretching before exercising could actually cause an injury as well as slowing you down. This is because stretching loosens muscles, which makes them less powerful and overall more prone to injury. Various research studies have concluded that stretching one part of the body can also lead to injury in another area that was not stretched. Also, it appears that competitive athletes who stretch as a warm–up activity can actually reduce the strength in their muscles by as much as 5.5 per cent as well as contributing to an overall feeling of weakness during the subsequent activity.

Instead, warm-ups should consist of exactly that – warming up the body. This means replicating the activity that you are about to undertake, so for tennis, start with gentle shuttle runs, building up the pace progressively, swing your arms, do high leg kicks, jog on the spot, do lunges, run with rapid changes of pace and direction, etc.

Save your stretching for the warm-down after tennis, as this will reduce soreness and ease the risk of a re-stiffening up of the joints. Your stretches should be gradual and held for a period of thirty seconds before release. A small, bouncing stretch routine is likely to introduce minute tears in muscle fibres and should be avoided. If you have access to one, an ice bath is marvellous for tired

You should never lose because you are not fit enough.

Tennis is a sport of suppleness, strength and agility.

muscles and makes a good addition to your warm-down routine.

Strength and Muscle Endurance

These are both necessary due to the demands made through continuous heavy action in one way – such as the serve, which puts pressure on the shoulder, the arm, the stomach and the back. Therefore, these muscle areas should be built up in order to cope with this strain.

There are any number of good strengthening programmes that may be worked out in your local gym using free weights or Nautilus-style equipment, but bear two notes of caution in mind. Firstly, it is easy to over-bulk muscles through overtraining to the point where it becomes counterproductive to tennis, and secondly, many sports clinicians now advise those athletes under sixteen years old to avoid heavy gym work using weights. This is because muscles can be overdeveloped in the adolescent body to the point where still-growing bones do not provide enough strength in the anchorage point for the muscle, thus leading to injury at this location.

Exercises such as sit-ups, chin pulls, step-ups, etc., are excellent strengthening aids. Also, make use of resistor elastic bands, which can be doubled over in order to provide an increased work load. A band tied to a door handle can be an excellent strengthening aid for (say) the service if you face away from the door and tension the band up and over your shoulder in a service action. Always try and replicate your stretching on the non-dominant side of your body as well, in order to keep your body in balance and thereby avoid the likelihood of injury.

Stamina

Tennis is a game primarily of explosive action, so stamina should not be a real problem if general health/fitness levels are good. Most games last on average no more than six points, and since thirty seconds are allowed between each point, with one and a half minutes' rest every other game, the occasions when stamina is really called into question, with long rallies over a long time period, are limited. However, they do happen and when they do you should be ready for them.

In the past, many top players obtained the bulk of their stamina training from on-court practice activities but today's pros augment their on-court time with similar spells in the gym. Where possible you should seek to train with an equal ratio of both steady-state and exhaustive work.

In steady-state you should try to maintain as high a work rate as possible without the need for rest periods, whereas in exhaustive work you should be prepared to work flat-out continuously for a period, take a short pause and then repeat the flat-out work, several times. A gym can help you in working out a suitable programme, but examples of steady-state work would include distance running and fartlek (variable pace) running, while for exhaustive work a shuttle run between the lines of the court is excellent, sprinting hard to touch each of the lines in succession, resting for thirty seconds and repeating the exercise three times.

KEY POINT

Fitness is not something that 'just happens'. It has to be worked at in all respects in order to get the maximum benefit possible from your game.

Speed

This is one of the most vital parts of the tennis player's armoury. The quicker you can get in place, the more time you have to achieve balance and control. Most top tennis players are gifted in this department, while others have to work at it. (It is said that Steffi Graf would have been one of the top four sprinters over 100 metres in Germany if she had concentrated on athletics rather than tennis.)

Taller players are sometimes said to have an actual physical problem to overcome in this area, as they often lack the explosive movement required, particularly from the legs. Explosive movement depends on the efficiency of muscles: how fast, far and for how long they will contract and stretch. Squat thrusts, tuck jumps, star jumps, alternate knee lifts, ladder work, etc., together with fast court-work practices, are all excellent for improving speed and agility.

Warm-Up and Warm-Down

Muscles perform more efficiently when warm as they become more relaxed and less prone to injury. Therefore, as described earlier, it is essential to include this activity as part of your normal court routine. Often, a hot shower is a good idea immediately before a match as a means of raising body temperature. Alternatively, you may try easy jogging combined with stretching and bending to touch the ground while doing so, combined with your own routine of match preparation.

It is probably true to say that the warm-up routine is one of the most commonly neglected tennis areas for the recreational player. I have often been struck by the number of players on public courts who will walk on, hit two or three half-hearted forehands and then suggest, 'OK, shall we play a set now?' Instead, make your warm-up work for you. It should be an opportunity to familiarize yourself with the court surface and your opponent as well as simple body preparation.

RULES CHECK

You are allowed a five-minute warm-up period before a match must start.

You should hit balls that vary in height, spin and pace, and note carefully how the court and your opponent handle them. Play all your strokes. Start at the baseline hitting half to three-quarter pace forehands, then backhands. Slowly move forwards, picking up some half-volleys ideally, to rally off both sides, again at half pace and always back to your opponent, utilizing him as a target. Ask for some overheads and, when you are happy, retreat and offer your opponent the same courtesies.

Gently warm up your service action with about ten deliveries to each side and at this stage, no less than before, concentrate fully on the impact point between racquet and ball. Stefan Edberg (ex-World No. 1) provided a good model in this respect. His very first warm-up serves were almost those of a beginner in their simplicity of action. His racquet was virtually placed behind his shoulder in advance, and a simple upwards throwing movement of the ball followed. There was virtually no preparation phase at all. Only when he was satisfied with this impact phase did he progress to a full service action.

On completion of your match, do not neglect the warm-down, as stiffening of joints will occur and the risk of injury will again be present. Ideally, jog some more, with more stretching and loosening, followed by a hot bath or shower and an ice bath. At the very least, get straight back into your tracksuit in order to allow your body to cool down gradually.

In this way, you should get more enjoyment from your tennis, and make it less necessary to have to refer to the next section.

CHAPTER 12

COMMON TENNIS INJURIES

If you have achieved a reasonable level of fitness and followed the suggestions previously made, you should not expect many injury problems on the tennis court. Tennis as a non-contact sport is no more or less dangerous in this aspect than many other activities, though you should always, of course, be sensible (and take particular care in doubles to avoid your partner's racquet). Beyond this, if you have not carried out any physical activity for a long time and are over thirty-five, or drastically over- or under-weight, take medical advice first. There is a careful balance to be determined between playing tennis to get fit, and getting fit to play tennis.

If, however, you have the misfortune to be injured, one of the simplest and most efficient remedies for a whole host of injuries is the technique of ice, rice and mice. 'I' stands for ice, 'C' stands for compression and 'E' for elevation. Thus rice, is rest, ice, compression, elevation and mice is movement, ice, compression and elevation.

On injury then, the affected body part should have ice applied for a five-minute period every hour, ideally over a 48-hour period. This will reduce bleeding from torn blood vessels and thus restrict bruising and reduce swelling. (A packet of frozen peas straight from the freezer makes an ideal ice-pack.) Compression is carried out by bandaging the affected areas sufficiently tightly to contain any swelling, while offering support and yet remaining comfortable. Elevation simply means that the limb should be raised. A leg should be supported by a chair, or an arm raised above the head. In this way, blood is allowed to flow towards the heart, and fluid pressure is reduced on the injury. Whether to allow rest (rice) or limited movement (mice) depends very much on the individual injury, and you should obviously take medical advice here. Some shoulder injuries, for instance, are actually made worse by immobility, and the joint should be gently exercised as a result.

Obviously, seek the advice of your doctor for all less obvious or protracted cases of injury, but it is worth remembering that specific sports injury treatment clinics exist to get you back competing again in the minimum amount of time. Medical General Practitioners are good as a first line of approach but they are unlikely to offer much more than the standard line of, 'Well, if it hurts when you play tennis, then don't play tennis.' A specialist sports injury clinic, however, will be more concerned with getting you treated or strapped in such a way that you can still compete, while rehabilitating your injury. If visiting a sports physiotherapist, do not delay too long while waiting to see if the injury improves. Prompt treatment for sports injuries will get you back playing again sooner.

Alternatively, many people have experienced positive results through visualization processes, such as imagining placing your hand in iced water until it feels numb. Once the numbness has been achieved, place your hand on the part of the body in pain. Imagine the coldness moving from your hand to the painful area, becoming colder and colder and then numb. Keep your hand on the area until all pain sensation is lost. Through visualizing their bodies actively healing an injury, many people claim to have markedly speeded up the healing process.

RULES CHECK

If you are injured while playing, you are allowed a three-minute rest period (or four-and-a-half minutes if it occurs at an end change).

Specific Tennis Injuries and Problems

Blisters

Blisters occur easily on feet through ill-fitting shoes or playing for long periods, or on the racquet hand through constant rubbing on the grip. If allowed to form a protective callus, this is no problem, but if the blister develops quickly and painfully it should be treated. To do this, clean with antiseptic, sterilize a needle by holding it in a flame until it is red hot and then allow it to cool. Prick the bubble allowing the fluid to escape, then, leaving the skin in place, cover with a gauze pad and adhesive tape.

Rigid Toe Injury

This may occur when the service action levers across the big toe of the back foot, causing pain to flare in the big toe joint. You should try and use a jump service action to minimize the stress on the joint.

Sprained Ankles

These are easily incurred, often by stepping on a stray ball and turning over on the ankle. Therefore, always make it a rule to ensure that loose balls are cleared from the playing area and immediately behind it. As a matter of courtesy, if a ball of yours rolls across or behind your neighbour's court, inform them immediately so they are not at risk. For treatment, use rice and avoid putting any weight on the ankle. Strap it when playing again until fully healed.

RULES CHECK

If the ball hits another ball on your side of the net and thus prevents you from making your return, you lose the point. It was your responsibility to clear the playing area of stray balls.

Calf Muscle Strain

This feels as if you have been struck hard on the back of the leg by a ball from another court, and often I have seen sufferers actually turn round and look for the cause of this sudden blow, only to try a step and realize then what has happened. The strain is caused by sudden overloading of the muscle, and the treatment is immediate: rice, especially compression. The injury normally takes about one to five weeks to heal.

Knees

The knee is the most injury-prone of all the joints, and takes an awful hammering on hard tennis courts. Torn cartilages may occur through sudden twisting movements, or over-use injuries may be caused. If the injury appears minor and responds to rice, fine; if not, seek immediate medical advice. It's possible that a scan will be necessary to diagnose the full extent of the injury.

Thigh Tears

Thigh tears may occur in the quads or hamstrings as a result of overloading the muscle, but these injuries are less frequent than in the calf area. If injury is caused to the leg muscles, the cause may well be inadequate training or warming up, and you should therefore modify your technique in these areas. For quick recovery, treatment is rice initially, then a gradual programme of stretching, leading into strengthening exercises.

Triceps Strain

This can occur when strain is caused by the sudden straightening of the elbow or by gripping the racquet too tightly between thumb and index finger, which prevents the wrist from releasing and causes the elbow to snap, thus aggravating the strain on the triceps. The answer is to loosen up, especially on the service action. Soreness, swelling and bruising in the forearm may also be caused by poor groundstrokes, or by over-use, or simply by using too heavy a racquet.

Wrist Strain

The wrist takes a lot of strain in tennis and tendon sheaths may be strained through over-use. Picking up a forehand so late that it is nearly past you can also be painful and lead to Pronator Terres Syndrome. There is obviously not a great deal you can do to prevent this, other than improve your technique and try not to allow the wrist to drop too much. In both situations use rice for treatment and utilize a proprietary brand wrist support when playing.

Tennis Elbow

Tennis elbow is a well-known injury that can be caused by something as simple as the action of turning a door handle or screwdriver. Overly tight strings or too large or too small a racquet grip can contribute to it, but the largest single cause is usually felt to be poor stroke technique, particularly on the backhand, where lack of an adequate shoulder turn often results in a push from the elbow (players who use two hands on the backhand seldom suffer from tennis elbow). If adequate strength training is not carried out, the injury can also be aggravated by the forehand when the open stance is adopted and the stroke takes place with lots of arm power and a minimum of shoulder rotation.

Any number of miracle cures exist on the open market for this injury and all have their sworn advocates. For longer-term treatment and pain relief, recognize first that this is an over-use injury, therefore use rice, avoid lifting any objects with the palm facing downwards, use a thicker pen for writing and, when you become pain-free, work on strengthening up the forearm muscles. Strapping and support will assist recovery by taking some of the load off the sore area.

Shoulder Strain

Like the knee, the shoulder joint has a wide range of movement and can take an awful lot of strain through over-use, resulting in tendonitis or bursitis. Poor technique may be the cause and you may feel a severe pain at the tip of the shoulder when you attempt to raise your arm. The answer is gentle movement plus ice in order to prevent the shoulder freezing up. (Of course, as in all injuries, if at all in doubt, seek medical advice.)

Neck Strains

This can be caused by a sudden awkward stretch or a serve made particularly when not thoroughly warmed up. Massage and the application of heat should help.

Lower Back

Older players may pull muscles or strain ligaments through the demands of constant bending and turning. Exercises for strengthening the lower back area are therefore useful and you should take advice from a sports injury specialist, osteopath, physiotherapist or chiropractor.

Abdominal Strain

This may occur as a result of poor technique on the serve or overhead; when overstretching happens, rice followed by gentle mobilization provides the treatment.

> TOP TIP
>
> 'Whenever I'm asked about a player's chances when going into a match with an injured shoulder or a pulled stomach muscle, my reply is always the same: if he goes out on court and stands behind that baseline, he's fit and ready to go. There are no excuses.'
>
> Fred Perry, *Autobiography* (Arrow, 1984).

Cramp and Stretches

These sudden, involuntary spasms, where the muscle suddenly tightens painfully and unexpectedly, are usually caused by overexertion, extreme cold which causes the muscle to tense, or extreme heat where the body loses salt through sweating. In the case of a stretch, the cause may be exerting oneself too soon after a meal. In very hot weather, when you are expecting to be on court a long time, add some salt to your on-court drink. Magnesium is a useful preventive measure, particularly when available in liquid form, which can be absorbed quickly into the bloodstream when taken thirty minutes before a match.

Heat Exhaustion

The 1988 Australian Open men's singles final was played in temperatures approaching 49°C (120°F), which is bordering on the very dangerous. However, the players managed through taking sensible precautions.

Wear a hat, drink plenty of liquids, and take salt tablets. (You may need to drink as much as three litres [five pints] of water during the course of a three-set match.) The aim is to allow the body to cool itself efficiently, as body temperatures above 38.9°C (102°F) will usually result in symptoms of cramps, tiredness and dizziness, while a temperature of 40.5°C (105°F) may cause unconsciousness, which counts as a full emergency as the body's cooling system has effectively shut down. At 41.7°C (107°F) body temperature, death will occur in a short period of time.

Sunburn: Take precautions and wear a high-factor sun protection cream, particularly on the face, and apply salve to your lips. Keep the back of your neck protected as much as possible.

CHAPTER 13

NUTRITION

In the same way that much more attention is nowadays paid to fitness training specifically for tennis, so more and more top players are turning to nutritionists in order to tune their bodies to the optimum level for top-flight performance.

As players develop younger and younger, there is often little consideration at this stage regarding a correct diet. Junk food is rapidly burned off through the twin mechanisms of physical exertion and natural body growth. It is after the body has reached maturity that a diet of junk food really starts harming the body. In recent years attention has correctly become focused on the important gains that can be achieved in tennis development, through dietary control.

Firstly, what is nutrition? A nutrient is a substance used by the body to keep itself going. It may have food value like protein, it may help muscle cells to function, like vitamins, or it may be vital for muscle cell life, like water.

Water and vitamins do not provide calories (which are a measure of the energy value of foods, and provide fuel for the body's functions) but they are equally vital. Without water, muscle cells do not function properly and the heart function decreases. Therefore, water lost through athletic performance must be constantly replaced, even in cold weather. While sports energy drinks are useful, most consist predominantly of water, therefore give your body what it really needs and wants – water! But be careful not to take too much, as this may result in the flushing away of important nutrients.

Minerals and vitamins are equally vital to nutrition as they improve the body's ability to do specific tasks by producing or speeding up chemical reactions. Fruit, vegetables and certain cereals, together with milk, provide a wide range of both vitamins and minerals and a good foundation to diet. If taking vitamin and mineral supplements, be careful not to overdose the body on them, as an excess can build up and become harmful.

Proteins, fats and carbohydrates are all important. Proteins are building blocks, vital for body maintenance and repair, and available in meat, poultry, fish, peas and beans, eggs and dairy produce. Fats are either saturated (from animals) or unsaturated (from vegetables). They provide a ready source of energy and provide structure for cell walls. All oils, butters and margarines are a ready source of fat. Carbohydrates are the first source of energy for cell function, and stored carbohydrate, called glycogen, is utilized for endurance activities. Sugar, cereal and potatoes all provide carbohydrate, together with fruit and vegetables, all of which are ideal for athletes as they take the least amount of time to pass through the stomach.

It is unwise to eat any foods less than an hour before competition. Especially avoid chocolate bars. Some players take these under the impression that they are receiving a quick energy boost, but they are in fact harmful as the result is low blood sugar and subsequent tiredness and weakness after the initial high.

Different theories have come and gone with regard to nutrition for tennis. In the 1960s and '70s it was very much the time of the high-protein diet, with players dining as often as not on steak, night after night. Current thinking, however, suggests that too much protein is converted in the body and stored as fat. In addition, too much can dehydrate a body because more frequent urination is necessary to rid the body of toxic protein by-products. As protein requires a lot of water, the body draws from working muscles and cells that need water most during athletic performance.

Provide your body with the fuel it needs for top performance.

Many nutritionists suggest cutting down on protein and increasing complex carbohydrates (including starches, potatoes, pasta, bread, vegetables, fruit and cereals). The theory is that these foods are quickly assimilated by the body, provide fast energy release and do not linger in the digestive system.

For some events, the practice of 'carbohydrate loading' may be used, whereby athletes overload on carbohydrate in order to store it in advance of requirement in muscles. By combining special diets and training programmes, the body may be 'tricked' into overstocking carbohydrate, which is slowly released throughout endurance events. Obviously, such manoeuvres should only be carried out under specific medical instruction.

Alcohol does not sit well with the nutritional needs of athletes. It is a diuretic, causing fluid loss, leading to dehydration which can decrease performance and lead to heatstroke. The empty calories provided are quickly turned to fat in the body, while cells are poisoned to the extent that damage to the liver, nervous system and brain are likely in the regular, heavy drinker. The long-term effect unfortunately is not reversible. For this reason, anything more than the occasional light social drink is not to be recommended for anyone wishing to play tennis well.

It is impossible to recommend the perfect diet for tennis players here, as so much depends on individual factors like weight, age, height, work rate, and so on. The ideal diet would provide an adequate mix of nutrients, including carbohydrates, vitamins, minerals, fats and proteins. These are to be found within the four basic food groups of dairy produce, fruit and vegetables, grains and meat. Obviously, the individual proportions will have to be recommended according to personal circumstances. (It is perfectly permissible to follow a vegetarian diet as an athlete, providing the imbalance in nutrients is made up elsewhere.)

A Suggested Approach to Tennis Diet

In Training

Always carry drinks and low fat snacks in your bag. Dried fruits are good, as are cereal bars. A wholemeal sandwich of tuna, cottage cheese, chicken or turkey is a good choice, but remember to spread butter or margarine thinly. Snack within half an hour to an hour after your training session.

Before Matches

Ensure your glycogen levels are high by slowly increasing your carbohydrates during the two days before a match. On the day before, choose pasta, rice or jacket potato for your main meal choice, supplemented with fresh fruit or low fat yoghurt. On the day of the match, if you're playing in the morning, have a light, high carbohydrate breakfast such as toast, cereal or fruit, while if your match is at midday, you can supplement breakfast with a mid-morning snack (fruit would be a good choice). If your match is in the afternoon, in addition to the breakfast and mid-morning snack, have a lunch of pasta or rice with bread, or a sandwich or roll (chicken or turkey) supplemented by low fat yoghurt or rice pudding.

After the Match

Try and eat a high carbohydrate meal within two hours as it takes around twenty hours to get muscle glycogen levels back to their optimal level. Stick to a normal well-balanced diet from then on. Remember to be careful when ordering food you are unfamiliar with, especially when travelling abroad. In conclusion, it should be reiterated that diet is extremely individual. As a result, individual advice should always be sought from specialists before attempting radical changes in life-style. It is also worth remembering (before this section is dismissed as being only of marginal interest) that the long-term effects of a correct diet are more important than just improving one's performance on the court.

If tennis is a sport for life, nutrition may be the key to extending the enjoyment of experience of that sport for the maximum period!

TOP TIP

'Proper diet and nutrition are a big part of being fit, but don't let the word 'diet' scare you. It doesn't mean you need to lose weight, but what you eat is very important. I stay away from fats, salt, sugar. I get my carbohydrates, 60–70 per cent of my diet, from pasta, potatoes, vegetables and salads. I get my protein from fish and poultry. Also, I cheat – everything in moderation. I get my occasional crepe Suzette and hot dog, but basically I know that what you eat will affect how you feel.'

Martina Navratilova (*Tennis*, 1990).

GLOSSARY

Ace	A ball served in such a way that it remains untouched by the opponent's return.
Backcourt	The area of the court behind the baseline.
Chip	Short chopping motion of the racquet against the back and bottom side of the ball.
Choking	To be overcome with nerves, seize up physically when a win is in sight.
Chopper	A grip.
Continental	A grip.
Dink	A very softly hit ball that floats over the net.
Eastern	A grip.
Grand Slam	To win the French, Wimbledon, the US and Australian championships back to back. (Some authorities insist that this should also be carried out within the same calendar year.)
Head	That part of the racquet that houses the strings.
Let	A point that is interfered with in some way, and needs to be replayed.
Mid-court	The area near the service line of the playing court.
Poach	To cross over into your partner's territory.
Propeller/windshield wiper drive	A high percentage attacking stroke. Heavy topspin is created by the racquet hitting across the face of the ball from a 4 o'clock position to a 9 o'clock one.
Rally	To maintain an exchange of strokes.
Service box	The area that the serve must fall within.
Tie-break	A game played specifically to break the deadlock encountered at 6 games all.
Western	A grip.

APPENDIX

USEFUL UK ADDRESSES

The International Tennis Federation
Bank Lane
Roehampton
London SW15 5XZ
United Kingdom
http://www.itftennis.com/
Telephone +44 (0)20 8878 6464
Fax +44 (0)20 8878 7799
Email communications@itftennis.com

Lawn Tennis Association
National Tennis Centre
100 Priory Lane
Roehampton
London SW15 5JQ
http://www.lta.org.uk/
Telephone +44 (0)20 8487 7000
Fax +44 (0)20 8487 7301
Email Info@LTA.org.uk

INDEX